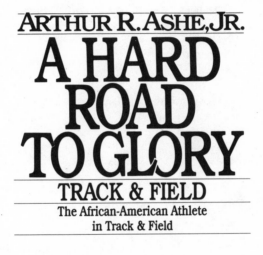

ARTHUR R. ASHE, JR.

A HARD ROAD TO GLORY

TRACK & FIELD

The African-American Athlete in Track & Field

Other titles in the *Hard Road to Glory* series

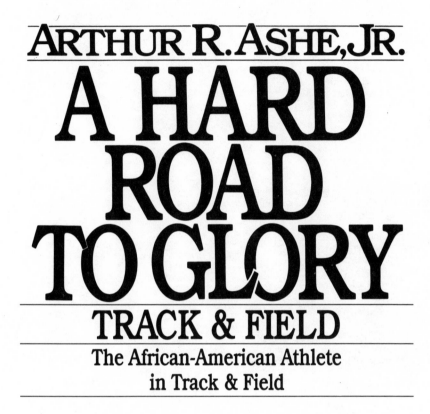

ARTHUR R. ASHE, JR.

A HARD ROAD TO GLORY

TRACK & FIELD

The African-American Athlete in Track & Field

WITH THE ASSISTANCE OF
KIP BRANCH, OCANIA CHALK, AND FRANCIS HARRIS

Amistad

NEW YORK, NEW YORK

"Views of Sport: Taking the Hard Road With Black Athletes" by Arthur R. Ashe, Jr., © 1988 by The New York Times Company. Reprinted by permission.

Amistad Press, Inc.
1271 Avenue of the Americas
New York, New York 10020

Distributed by:
Penguin USA
375 Hudson Street
New York, New York 10014

Produced by March Tenth, Inc.

1   2   3   4   5   6   7   8   9   10

Library of Congress Cataloging-in-Publication Data
Ashe, Arthur.
    A hard road to glory—track & field : the African-American athlete in track & field / Arthur R. Ashe, Jr. ; with the assistance of Kip Branch, Ocania Chalk, and Francis Harris.
        p.   cm.
    "The text of this book was taken from the three-volume set of A hard road to glory and combined into one compendium on track & field"—CIP data sheet.
    ISBN 1-56743-039-2 : $9.95
    1. Track-athletics—United States—History.   2. Afro-American athletes—– Statistics.   I. Ashe, Arthur.   Hard road to glory. II. Title.
GV1060.6.A84   1993
796.42'0973—dc20   93-37952
                                                     CIP

Contents

To my wife, Jeanne, and my daughter, Camera

Publisher's Statement

The untimely passing of Arthur Ashe on February 6, 1993, requires telling the story of how *A Hard Road to Glory* came to be. It is a story that echoes its title, a tale that takes place in the publishing world and yet, not surprisingly, contains similar elements to those found in the world of sports: extraordinary individual effort, unified teamwork, setbacks, defeats, and eventual victory. It is only a partial testimony to a courageous man whom I was proud to have as a colleague and a friend.

Ten years earlier, in February 1983, while I was executive director of Howard University Press in Washington, DC, I received a telephone call from Arthur Ashe. He had heard of my interest in seeing that a work on the history of the Black athlete be published. He had expressed a similar desire to Marie Brown, a literary agent, who had referred him to me. He asked me when I planned to visit New York City again, and I told him it just so happened that I had to be there the next day.

That was not completely true. However, this subject was of such burning interest to me and I was so excited that a person of Arthur's stature was interested in writing such a book that I felt I should move expeditiously.

The following day I met him at his apartment on East 72nd Street, where we had a brief discussion. Then we went to his agent,

Fifi Oscard, and met with her and Kevin McShane of the Oscard Agency. Arthur presented a general outline of the book that became the basis of our discussion, which in turn led to the negotiation of a contract.

On April 5, 1983, with the approval of the Executive Committee of the Commission on Management and Operations of Howard University Press, we formally executed a contract for a book that was tentatively titled *A History of the Black Athlete in America.* In May 1983 Arthur came to Washington, where we held a press conference and a ceremonial signing of the contract at the Palm Restaurant. I felt ecstatic that we were making the kind of history that would influence generations.

It should be noted that Arthur came to Howard University Press because, of the more than twenty commercial publishers in New York that he had approached, not one had seen the value or viability of a book on the history of Black athletes.

As he was soon to learn, however, Arthur and I had much more in common. We shared similar backgrounds of growing up in Virginia: He was from Richmond and I am from Portsmouth. We both attended schools (Maggie L. Walker High School and I. C. Norcom High School) that although segregated had outstanding teachers who nurtured Black students, instilled in them the desire to achieve, and provided important contacts to do so in the wider world. We were proud to be working together.

In June 1983, Arthur underwent double-bypass heart surgery. Miraculously, in a matter of weeks he was back at work on this project. His commitment went far beyond intellectual curiosity and enthusiasm. By this time Arthur had already assembled the nucleus of his research team, which included Ocania Chalk, Kip Branch, Derilene McCloud, and Sandra Jamison. (Rod Howard later replaced Ms. Jamison.) My son Francis Harris was to join this team in September 1983. (Doug Smith, of *USA Today*, assisted in this edition.)

In December 1985, I resigned from my position at Howard University Press, effective June 1986. I then began the preliminary stages of forming Amistad Press, Inc. as an independent publishing house managed and controlled by African Americans. After fifteen years at a university press, which had followed fifteen years with commercial publishers in New York, I was ready to move on to the professional challenge of my life.

There were still, however, some loose ends at Howard. Sensing a lack of scholarly and administrative support, Arthur asked university officials in January 1986 if they still had a commitment to publish his book. Within twenty-four hours of his question he was informed by an officer of the university that they had no further interest in his work. They were agreeable to his finding another publisher, and on February 21, 1986, Howard University released Arthur from his contract. By this time he had compiled about 75 percent of the material found in the present volumes. It was inconceivable that the project should stop at this point. We had come too far.

Arthur and I agreed that he would explore opportunities with other publishing houses

for his work while I was attempting to raise capital to launch Amistad Press. In May 1986, I met Lynne Lumsden and Jon Harden, who had recently purchased Dodd, Mead and Company, Inc., a venerable New York firm with a reputation for publishing influential African-American authors. We began negotiations for a joint venture in book publishing. By the middle of June 1986, we had settled on the legal parameters for this relationship. On July 1, 1986, Amistad Press, Inc. was incorporated in the State of New York. On August 22, 1986, Arthur Ashe signed a contract with Dodd, Mead and Amistad Press to publish *A Hard Road to Glory: A History of the African-American Athlete.* He had decided on this evocative title, and we all agreed that the work, based on original and extensive research, would necessarily consist of several volumes.

The entire team was working well. We had negotiated another critical turn in the development of this project, and we were feeling elated, for we had finally found a supportive atmosphere in the private sector. We shared an enthusiasm and a commitment to see this work through to its successful publication.

We planned to publish the work in the fall of 1987. To this end, Arthur appeared on the Author's Breakfast Program of the annual meeting of the American Booksellers Association, which was held in Washington, DC, at the end of May.

A Hard Road to Glory was announced with great fanfare and extensive promotional material, and it was received with equally positive interest.

In November 1987, while we were furiously engaged in the tasks of copyediting, proofreading, and typesetting, we learned that Dodd, Mead was experiencing financial difficulty. By February 1988, when it was confirmed that Dodd, Mead would not be able to proceed with this project, Amistad was offered the opportunity to purchase the Dodd,

Mead interest in the contracts that we owned jointly, including that of *A Hard Road to Glory*. I accepted with great pleasure and some trepidation. We still had to find a way to get the books out.

I initiated discussions with several publishing houses to explore their interests in a joint venture relationship similar to the one that Amistad had had with Dodd, Mead. In the spring of 1988 discussions began with Larry Kirshbaum, president of Warner Books. Simultaneously, through the efforts of Clarence Avant, I met Martin D. Payson, who at the time was general counsel of Warner Communications, Inc., which owned Warner Books. Marty Payson, who worked closely with Warner Communications's chairman, Steve Ross, became enthralled with the idea of *A Hard Road to Glory* and thought it would be a significant project for Warner Books and Warner Communications. A joint venture between Amistad Press and Warner Books began in April 1988. We then set a new publication date for November. Our spirits were lifted again.

While completing the final stages of reviewing galleys and sample page proofs, Arthur began having trouble using his right hand. Ultimately, he underwent brain surgery. As a result of this operation, he learned that he had been infected with HIV, the virus which was to take his life.

The publication of *A Hard Road to Glory* was a major achievement for a man who had had many triumphs. Arthur was intimately involved in the work at every stage of its development, from proposal to manuscript to bound books. He had been released from the hospital only a few days before the books arrived from the printer in October 1988. He asked his wife, Jeanne, to drive him from their home in Mt. Kisco, New York, to my apartment in Manhattan, where he saw the finished copies for the first time.

The first books had come from the bindery on a Friday and were sent directly to my home so that I would not have to wait until Monday to see them. I had received the books on Saturday, when I telephoned Arthur. His first reaction upon seeing them was similar to mine: He simply stared at them. We both looked at each other and smiled continuously. Because their daughter, Camera, was asleep, Jeanne had remained in the car and waited until my wife, Sammie, and I came back with Arthur and his first set of books. I think we were all nearly speechless because we realized what a tremendous ordeal and success we had experienced together.

This edition of *A Hard Road to Glory* names a single publisher of the work, Amistad Press, Inc. My wife and I started this company with our own personal financial resources. We were able to keep the company going in lean early years because Arthur became the first outside investor and supported us in attracting other investors. He personally guaranteed a bank loan that had been difficult to obtain, since the company had not yet published any books. Fortunately, we paid off that loan many years ago. Through Arthur's efforts we were able not only to publish his work, but we were also able to bring other important works to the public. We are on the road to achieving the goals for which Amistad Press was founded.

Present and future generations of writers will owe a great debt to a great man, Arthur R. Ashe, Jr., for helping make it possible for them to have a platform from which to present their creativity to the world.

Charles F. Harris
President and Publisher
Amistad Press, Inc.
March 1993

Views of Sport:

Taking the Hard Road With Black Athletes

by Arthur R. Ashe, Jr.

My three-volume book, *A Hard Road to Glory: A History of the African-American Athlete*, began almost as an afterthought to a seminar class I was asked to give on the historical and sociological role of the African-American athlete. Though I had never seen it, I assumed some esteemed black historian, sociologist or sports reporter had compiled the entire story of the black athlete in one volume. A search found only "The Negro in Sports," by Edwin B. Henderson, written in 1938 and slightly updated in 1948.

After three months of preliminary research, three inhibiting factors emerged for anyone wishing to put it all together: it would take more money than any reasonable publisher's advance would cover; black historians never deemed sports serious enough for their scarce time; and these same historians had underestimated the socio-historical impact of the black athlete in black American life. But the truth is that the psychic value of success in sports was and is higher in the black community than among any other American subculture.

This high psychic reward is not a contemporary phenomenon. Just after the Civil War when sports clubs were formed and rules were written, athletes became the most well known and among the richest of black Americans. Isaac Murphy, perhaps the greatest American jockey of the 19th century, earned more than $25,000. A black newspaper, the Baltimore Afro-American, complained in an editorial in 1902 that Joe Gans, the black world lightweight boxing champion, got more publicity than Booker T. Washington. It is no different today; Mike Tyson is better known around the world than Jesse Jackson.

In spite of the obstacles, I decided to proceed with the book because I became obsessed with so many unanswered questions. How did black America manage to create such a favorable environment for its athletes? Why did so many blacks excel so early on with so little training, poor facilities and mediocre coaching? Why did the civil rights organizations of the time complain so little about the discrimination against black athletes? And why were white athletes so afraid of competing on an equal basis with blacks? I just had to have my own answers to these and other puzzling sets of facts.

For 120 years, white America has gone to extraordinary lengths to discredit and discourage black participation in sports because black athletes have been so accomplished. The saddest case is that of the black jockeys. When the first Kentucky Derby was run in 1875, 15 thoroughbreds were entered and 14 of their riders were black. Black domination of horse racing then was analogous to the domination of the National Basketball Association today. Subsequently, the Jockey Club was formed in the early 1890's to regulate and license all jockeys. Then one by one the blacks were denied their license renewals. By 1911 they had all but disappeared.

This example appears in Volume I, which covers the years 1619–1918. It is the slimmest of the three volumes but took the most time, effort and cross-referencing of facts. Starting with official record books of all the sports, I sought to find out who was black, where he (there was no appreciable female involvement until World War I) came from, and where he learned his skills. I encountered two major obstacles: no American or world record was recognized unless it was under the auspices of a white college or the Amateur Athletic Union (simply put, no records set at black colleges or black club events counted to national or international governing bodies); and some early black newspapers published accounts that were frequently, if unintentionally, just plain wrong.

In the 27 years between the end of the two World Wars (the period covered by Volume II), the foundation for the quantum leaps made by black athletes after 1950 was laid. Again there were several cogent factors that influenced both the pace and progress of the black athlete. The one institution that provided minimum competition and facilities was the black college. But many of these schools still had white presidents and the small cadre of black presidents were hesitant to spend money on athletics for fear of alienating white donors who may have preferred an emphasis on academics.

A very positive factor was the formation of the black college conferences. But to white America, these conferences were nearly non-entities. They never got to see Alfred (Jazz) Bird of Lincoln University in Pennsylvania, or Ben Stevenson of Tuskegee Institute, who is by consensus the greatest black college football player before World War II. They never saw Ora Washington of Philadelphia, who may have been the best female athlete ever. Of course everyone knew and saw Jack Johnson, Jesse Owens and Joe Louis. They were, and still are, household names.

There were other famous names who because of their own naivete, bitterness and ignorance suffered indignities that brought me and my staff to tears of sadness and tears of rage. In 1805, for example, according to an account in The Times of London, Tom Molineaux, a black American from Richmond, Va., actually won the English (and world) heavyweight boxing title in the 27th round against Tom Cribb, but the paper quotes the English referee as saying to the prostrate Cribb, "Get up Tom, don't let the nigger win." Cribb was given four extra minutes to recover and eventually won.

. . .

There were times, to be sure, when white America got a glimpse of our premiere black athletes. The first black All-American football player, William H. Lewis, surfaced in 1892. Lewis was followed 25 years later by Paul Robeson and Fritz Pollard. But the most heralded confrontations took place on the baseball diamond when black teams played white major league all-star aggregations. The black squads won almost 75 percent of the time. The same for basketball. In the late 1920's and 1930's the original Celtics refused to join the whites-only professional leagues so they could continue to play against two black teams: the New York Rens and the Harlem Globetrotters.

Between 1945 and 1950, the athletic establishment was upended when all the major sports were integrated, in some places. What the black athlete did in the next 38 years is nothing less than stupendous. In particular, he (and she) brought speed to every activity. With fewer and fewer exceptions, whites were not to be seen in the sprints on the tracks or in the backfield on the gridiron.

Which brings us to the primary unanswered question of the project. Do black Americans have some genetic edge in physical activities involving running and jumping? My reply is that nature, our unique history in America, and our exclusion from other occupations have produced the psychic addiction to success in sports and entertainment. Once the momentum was established, continuing success became a matter of cultural pride. And yes, we do feel certain positions in sports belong to us. Quick, name a white halfback in the National Football League? Who was the last white sprinter to run 100 meters under 10 seconds?

Records aside, black athletes have had a major impact on black American history. In the early 1940's, for example, the black labor leader A. Phillip Randolph made the integration of major league baseball a test of the nation's intentions regarding discrimination in employment. The phrase "If he's [a black man] good enough for the Navy, he's good enough for the majors" became an oft-heard slogan for many. And when the opportunity finally came, it seemed almost predictable that black America would produce a Jim Brown, a Wilt Chamberlain, an Althea Gibson, a Bill Russell, a Gale Sayers, a Muhammed Ali, a Lee Evans, a Carl Lewis, and yes, a Tommie Smith and a John Carlos.

Proportionately, the black athlete has been more successful than any other group in any other endeavor in American life. And he and she did it despite legal and social discrimination that would have dampened the ardor of most participants. The relative domination of blacks in American sports will continue into the foreseeable future. Enough momentum has been attained to insure maximum sacrifice for athletic glory. Now is the time for our esteemed sports historians to take another hard look at our early athletic life, and revise what is at present an incomplete version of what really took place.

This essay first appeared in the New York Times *on Sunday, November 13, 1988, one day before* A Hard Road to Glory *was first published. We reprint it here as Arthur Ashe's reflections on the necessity and significance of this work.*

Foreword

When a discussion arises about athletes as role models, the argument invariably focuses on professional baseball, basketball, and football players. Ironically, perhaps the best athletic role models in the country—track and field stars—are omitted from the discussion.

Long before basketball, baseball, and football began accepting Black players in their professional ranks, African-American athletes excelled in track and field. As early as 1904, George Poage, a University of Wisconsin graduate, received the bronze medal in the 400-meter hurdles at that year's Olympics. John Taylor, the first African American to win an Olympic gold medal, did it in 1908.

Many of the African-American athletes of that period graduated from the East and Midwest's most prestigious schools and went on to establish professional careers.

Perhaps the most outstanding role model of the 1930s was Jesse Owens. Owens, incredibly, won four gold medals in the 1936 Olympics: for the 100 meters, 200 meters, 4 × 100 meters-relay, and long jump. Second to Owens in the 100 meters, winning a silver medal, was Ralph Metcalfe; winning silver in the 200 meters was Mack Robinson, Jackie's brother.

It is often forgotten that in the 1936 Olym-pics, with Owens, was a contingent of stellar African-American athletes. Cornelius Johnson and Dave Albritton won gold and silver med-als, respectively, in the high jump; Archie Williams and James Luvalle earned gold and bronze in the 400 meters; John Woodruff won a gold in the 800 meters; and Fritz Pollard, Jr. claimed a bronze in the 110-meter hurdles.

Yet, in spite of such brilliant performances by these athletes, Americans (not to exclude African Americans) tend to treat track and field stars the way they treat Jazz artists—as an afterthought. Jazz, the only true American music form, was created by Black musicians, and some of its best practitioners still are African Americans. Yet, this music is not the mainstay of our Black—or White, for that matter—communities. It is most prized, and appreciated, by Europeans. The same is true for Black athletes in track and field.

Two years ago, I interviewed Roger King-dom, an Olympic gold medalist and world record holder in the 110-meter hurdles. Kingdom was recuperating from knee surgery and contemplating a comeback. While we were seated in a restaurant, our waiter noticed my pen, pad, and micro-recorder. He studied Kingdom's physique and concluded that he was an athlete. But whom? Because we were in Pittsburgh, he guessed that Kingdom was a receiver for the Steelers, or, perhaps, an outfielder for the Pirates. Kingdom and I grinned at the puzzled look on the waiter's face. Bemused, Kingdom said he couldn't walk any place in Europe without being recognized and mobbed for his autograph. He could have walked through any neighborhood in Pittsburgh and probably gone unrecognized.

Just as Michael Jordan and Roger Craig are top-notch athletes, so too are Michael Johnson and Roger Kingdom. All of them deserve recognition.

The media, however, seem to slight those in track and field. Bob Beamon caught the world by surprise with his record-shattering long jump in the 1968 Olympics. It so exceeded the existing world record that many sports analysts claimed it to be the sport's achievement of the century. Beamon held the record for almost a quarter century until Mike Powell broke it in 1992. The media struggled to find videotape of Powell's victory—it was not televised. This modern-day neglect of track and field probably has more to do with economics than race. The gate receipts for basketball, baseball, or football exceed those of track by tens of millions of dollars. This does not, however, negate the importance of those athletes in track and field, or their importance in motivating and inspiring others. This volume dramatically points that out.

What young girl wasn't inspired by Wilma Rudolph, who overcame polio as a child and went on to win three Olympic gold medals? Nell Jackson, coach of the 1956 women's Olympic team, said that "Wilma's accomplishments opened up the real door for women in track because of her grace and beauty. People saw her as beauty in motion."

What athlete was not inspired by Gail Devers, who overcame Graves disease and won two medals in the 1992 Olympics? And who is not inspired by the strength, determination, and intelligence of Jackie Joyner-Kersee?

The success of these women in track did not come easy. They were continuing a legacy built by such stalwarts as Alice Coachman who won seven consecutive national Amateur Athletic Union (AAU) championships (1939–1945) in the high jump. Coach Ed Temple at Tennessee State, who retired earlier this year, built his teams into a dominant force in track and field throughout the world in the 1950s and 1960s. Several of his teams set world records and, besides Rudolph, he developed such stars as Mae Faggs, Edith McGuire, Madeline Manning, and Wyomia Tyus.

But before Temple and Tennessee State there was Cleveland Abbott and Tuskegee. Tuskegee was the major national force in women's track during the 1940s.

Often, journalists make it seem as though Black athletes, like Topsy, "just grew" into Olympic caliber performers; as if all they needed was to be born Black and a chance to run. The Black track and field athletes have trained, tinkered with technique, maintained strict diets, and endured many injuries on the road to glory. The athletes in track and field cannot depend on a teammate to pick up the slack; they cannot look to the next game, the playoffs, or next season to redeem themselves for a bad performance. With these athletes the future is always now. The challenge is always just hours or seconds away. The challenger is the clock or the measuring tape. They are out there alone, with but a few moments to capitalize on a lifetime's worth of preparation.

So often, sports is dismissed as show-and-tell in Black history. Without the contributions of Black track and field stars, many opportunities for other Black students may not have surfaced at prestigious universities. Arthur Ashe understood this perhaps better than anyone. In this volume of *A Hard Road to Glory*, he goes beyond the familiar stories of Owens and Rudolph and takes us from a slave's hunger to run, to Gail Devers's desire to compete.

There is much to gain from studying the history of African-American athletes in track and field. Their struggle parallels the civil rights movement. Just as we have overcome, but not yet arrived, the Black athlete continues to make strides in track and field as coaches, agents, trainers, and administrators. Thanks to Arthur Ashe for telling us their story.

Merlisa Lawrence
October 1993

Merlisa Lawrence is a reporter at *Sports Illustrated* magazine. She has also worked on the sports beat for the *Pittsburgh Press* and *Tampa Tribune*.

Foreword

TO

A Hard Road to Glory:
A History of the African-American Athlete, Volumes 1–3

This book began in a classroom at Florida Memorial College in Miami, Florida, in 1981. I was asked to teach a course, The Black Athlete in Contemporary Society, by Jefferson Rogers of the school's Center for Community Change. When I tried to find a book detailing what has surely been the African-American's most startling saga of successes, I found that the last attempt had been made exactly twenty years before.

I then felt compelled to write this story, for I literally grew up on a sports field. My father was the caretaker of the largest public park for blacks in Richmond, Virginia. Set out in a fanlike pattern at Brookfield Playground was an Olympic-size pool, a basketball court, four tennis courts, three baseball diamonds, and two football fields. Our five-room home was actually on these premises. Little wonder I later became a professional athlete.

My boyhood idol was Jackie Robinson, as was the case with every black kid in America in the late 1940s and early 1950s. But I had no appreciation of what he went through or, more importantly, what others like him had endured. I had never heard of Jack Johnson, Marshall Taylor, Isaac Murphy, or Howard P. Drew—icons in athletics but seldom heralded in the post-World War II period.

These and others have been the most accomplished figures in the African-American subculture. They were vastly better known in their times than people such as Booker T. Washington, William E.B. Du Bois, or Marcus Garvey. They inspired idolatry bordering on deification, and thousands more wanted to follow. Indeed, in the pretelevision days of radio, Joe Louis's bouts occasioned impromptu celebration because, between 1934 and 1949, Louis lost only once.

But if contemporary black athletes' exploits are more well known, few fully appreciate their true Hard Road to Glory. Discrimination, vilification, incarceration, dissipation, ruination, and ultimate despair have dogged the steps of the mightiest of these heroes. And, only a handful in the last 179 years have been able to live out their post-athletic lives in peace and prosperity.

This book traces the development of African-American athletes from their ancestral African homelands in the seventeenth century through the present era. Their exploits are explored in a historical context, as all African-American successes were constrained by discriminatory laws, customs, and traditions.

As I began to complete my research, I realized that the subject was more extensive than I had thought. All of the material would

xxi

not fit into one volume. Therefore, I have divided the work as follows:

Volume I covers the emergence of sports as adjuncts to daily life from the time of ancient civilizations like Egypt through World War I. Wars tend to compartmentalize eras and this story is no different. Major successes of African-Americans occurred in the nineteenth century, for example, which are simply glossed over in most examinations of the period.

Volume II examines black athletics during that vital twenty-year period between the World Wars. No greater contrast exists than that between the 1920s—the Golden Decade of Sports—and the Depression-plagued 1930s. The infrastructure of American athletics as we know it today was set during these crucial years, and the civil rights apparatus that would lead to integration in the post–World War II era was formalized. Popular African-American literature and its press augmented the already cosmic fame of athletes such as Jesse Owens and Joe Louis, who were the first black athletes to be admired by all Americans.

Volume III is set between World War II and the present. It begins with an unprecedented five-year period—1946 through 1950—in which football, baseball, basketball, tennis, golf, and bowling became integrated. These breakthroughs, coupled with the already heady showings in track and boxing, provided enough incentive for African-Americans to embark on nothing less than an all-out effort for athletic fame and fortune.

The reference sections in each volume document the major successes of these gladiators. These records are proof positive of effort and dedication on the playing field. More importantly, they are proof of what the African-American can do when allowed to compete equally in a framework governed by a set of rules.

Each volume is divided into individual sport histories. Primary source materials were not to be found in the local public library and not even in New York City's Fifth Avenue Public Library. Chroniclers of America's early sports heroes simply left out most of their darker brothers and sisters except when they participated in white-controlled events. Much had to be gleaned, therefore, from the basements, attics, and closets of African-Americans themselves.

Interviews were invaluable in cross-referencing dubious written records. Where discrepancies occurred, I have stated so; but I have tried to reach the most logical conclusion. Some unintentional errors are inevitable. The author welcomes confirmed corrections and additions. If validated, they will be included in the next edition of this work.

Today, thousands of young African-Americans continue to seek their places in the sun through athletics. For some African-Americans the dream has bordered on a pathological obsession. But unless matters change, the majority may end up like their predecessors. Perhaps this history will ease the journey with sober reflections of how difficult and improbable the Hard Road really is. In no way, however, do I care to dissuade any young athlete from dreaming of athletic glory. Surely every American at some time has done so.

A word about nomenclature. Sociologists have referred to nearly all immigrant groups in hyphenated form: Irish-Americans, Italian-Americans, and Jewish-Americans. African-Americans are no different, and this term is correct. Throughout this book, I shall, however, use the modern designation *"black"* to refer to African-Americans. The appellations *Negro* and *colored* may also appear, but usually in quotes and only when I thought such usage may be more appropriate in a particular context.

November 1988

Acknowledgments

A Hard Road to Glory would have been impossible without the help, assistance, contributions, and encouragement of many people. Initial moral support came from Reverend Jefferson Rogers, formerly of Florida Memorial College; Professor Henry Louis "Skip" Gates of Cornell University; Howard Cosell; Marie Brown; my editor, Charles F. Harris; and my literary agent, Fifi Oscard. All made me believe it could be done. An inspiring letter urging me to press on also came from Professor John Hope Franklin of Duke University, who advised that this body of work was needed to fill a gap in African-American history.

My staff has been loyal and faithful to the end these past four years. I have been more than ably assisted by Kip Branch, who has stood by me from the first day; and by Ocania Chalk, whose two previous books on black collegiate athletes and other black athletic pioneers provided so much of the core material for *A Hard Road to Glory*. To my personal assistant, Derilene McCloud, go special thanks for coordinating, typing, filing, phoning, and organizing the information and interviews, as well as keeping my day-to-day affairs in order. Sandra Jamison's skills in library science were invaluable in the beginning. Her successor, Rod Howard, is now a virtual walking encyclopedia of information about black athletes, especially those in college. To Francis Harris, who almost single-handedly constructed the reference sections, I am truly grateful. And to Deborah McRae, who sat through hundreds of hours of typing—her assistance is not forgotten.

Institutions have been very helpful and forthcoming. The people at the New York Public Annex went out of their way to search for books. *The New York Times* provided access to back issues. The Norfolk, Virginia, Public Library was kind and considerate. This book could not have been done without the kind help of the Schomburg Library for Research in Black Culture in Harlem, New York. Its photography curator, Deborah Willis Thomas, found many photographs for me, and Ernest Kaiser followed my work with interest.

The Enoch Pratt Free Library in Baltimore, Maryland; the Moorland-Spingarn Library at Howard University in Washington, D.C.; and the Library of Congress not only assisted but were encouraging and courteous. The offices of the Central Intercollegiate Athletic Association, the Southern Intercollegiate Athletic Conference, the Mideastern Athletic Conference, and the Southwestern Athletic Conference dug deep to find information on past black college sports. The National Collegiate Athletic Association and the National Association for Intercollegiate Athletics were quick with information about past and present athletes. The home offices of major league baseball, the National Basketball Association, the National Football League, and their archivists and Halls of Fame were eager to provide assistance. Joe Corrigan went out of his way to lend a hand.

The staffs at Tuskegee University and Tennessee State University were particularly kind. Wallace Jackson at Alabama A&M was helpful with information on the Southern Intercollegiate Athletic Conference. Alvin Hollins at Florida A&M University was eager to assist. Lynn Abraham of New York City found a rare set of boxing books for me. Lou Robinson of Claremont, California, came through in a pinch with information on black Olympians, and Margaret Gordon of the American Tennis Association offered her assistance.

Many people offered to be interviewed for this project—especially Eyre Saitch, Nell Jackson, Dr. Reginald Weir and Ric Roberts—and I am truly grateful for their recollections. (Eyre Saitch and Ric Roberts have since passed away.) Others who agreed to sit and talk with Kip Branch, Ocania Chalk, or me include William "Pop" Gates, Elgin Baylor, Oscar Robertson, Anita DeFranz, Nikki Franke, Peter Westbrook, Paul Robeson, Jr., Afro-American sportswriter Sam Lacy, A.S. "Doc" Young, Frederick "Fritz" Pollard, Jr., Mel Glover, Calvin Peete, Oscar Johnson, Althea Gibson, Mrs. Ted Paige, Charles Sifford, Howard Gentry, Milt Campbell, Otis Troupe, Beau Jack, Coach and Mrs. Jake Gaither, Lynn Swann, Franco Harris, Dr. Richard Long of Atlanta University, Dr. Leonard Jeffries of the City College of New York, Dr. Elliot Skinner of Columbia University, and Dr. Ben Jochannon.

Dr. Maulana Karenga of Los Angeles and Dr. William J. Baker of the University of Maine offered material and guidance on African sports. Dr. Ofuatey Kodjo of Queens College in New York City helped edit this same information. Norris Horton of the United Golfers Association provided records, and Margaret Lee of the National Bowling Association answered every inquiry with interest. To Nick Seitz of *Golf Digest* and *Tennis*, I offer thanks for his efforts. Professors Barbara Cooke, Patsy B. Perry, Kenneth Chambers, Floyd Ferebee, and Tom Scheft of North Carolina Central University were kind enough to read parts of the manuscript, as did Mr. and Mrs. Donald Baker. Professor Eugene Beecher of Wilson College, an unabashed sports fan, shuttled many clippings our way.

To the dozens of people who heard about my book on Bob Law's *Night Talk* radio show and sent unsolicited but extremely valuable information, I cannot thank you enough. And to the hundreds of unsung African-American athletes who played under conditions of segregation and whose skills and talents were never known to the general public, I salute you and hope this body of work in some measure vindicates and redresses that gross miscarriage of our American ideals.

Finally, to my wife Jeanne Moutoussamy-Ashe, I owe gratitude and tremendous appreciation for her understanding, patience, tolerance, and sacrifice of time so I could complete this book.

Arthur R. Ashe, Jr.
1988

CHAPTER 1

The Beginnings to 1918

Early History

Running for some people today seems genetically programmed. They must run, jog, amble, or mope along, or else they will suffer psychological damage. Ancient man *had* to run, or he would not have eaten. Survival depended on the swiftness of some of those prehistoric tribesmen. Consequently, nearly every society has prized its fleetest runners, and even monarchs have been known to try it as sport. King Amenophis II of Egypt (c. 1438 B.C.) was a skilled archer, strong rower, and swift runner. Perhaps the most famous example is Phidippides, the messenger who ran twenty-six miles from the plains of Marathon to tell his countrymen of victory in battle.

At the Olympic Games in pre-Christian Greece, the ideal athlete was the winner of the five-event pentathlon, of which two were field activities—javelin and discus— and the other a 200-meter dash. The very first event in that first Olympics in 776 B.C. was a foot race of approximately 200 meters.

African runners were familiar to these Greeks. The historian Herodotus referred to the athletic skills of "Aethiopians" (the Greek word for all Africans at one time) in saying they were "exceedingly fleet of foot—more so than any people of whom we have information."[1] Herodotus probably had in mind the Africans of the savannah grasslands, who indeed had to run great distances to hunt game. Hunting parties were honored in their villages, and training runs were held to determine who could withstand their rigors. In all but the most densely vegetated parts of Africa, the swiftest and strongest runners were not only honored but necessary for group survival.

As late as the 1930s, French anthropologist Charles Beart mentioned what he thought was a wondrous phenomenon. He lived in Ougadougou (now in Burkina Faso) and thought it faster to send a package to Niamey by an African porter than by mail.

African slaves brought this love of running, and jumping and their natural swiftness to America and engaged in many races among themselves. (Here they encountered Native Americans, who shared their love of running. Some Native American tribes made fleetness a standard part of their rites of passage for young males.) Girls ran, too, as had their African ancestors. The passage of time and assimilation into European customs did not dim

1

this craving: "most slave children thought of themselves as skillful 'athletes'; their white counterparts were generally felt to be less competent physically, unable to dance, run, jump, or throw."[2]

William Johnson, the free black barber who kept a diary from 1835 until 1852, wrote of frolicking with his sons. "I made a jump or 2 with the boys this Evening and beat Bill Nix about six inches in a one-half hamon Jump." (A hamon jump was a jump with no running start.) Ex-slave and civil rights leader Frederick Douglass wrote in his autobiography that "the majority [of slaves] spent the holidays in sports, ball-playing, wrestling, boxing, foot racing.[3] Even the intellectual William E. B. DuBois mentioned in his book *The Souls Of Black Folk* the elation a black boy felt at defeating a white boy in a foot race when he had no other way to assert himself.

But not all racing activities before the Emancipation Proclamation banned blacks. The Highland Games, organized by some Scottish-American groups, welcomed blacks, and the YMCAs organized events at their Colored branches as early as 1853. There were also professional walking races—"pedestrianism," as it was called—in the period from the 1830s to the 1880s. The horse-drawn trolleys in New York City made pedestrianism one of the first mass-attendance sports in the country along with boat racing. Francis Smith in the 1830s and Frank Hart in the 1870s were noted black walkers.

These early walking and running events usually pitted one ethnic group against another for prizes approaching a thousand dollars. Promoters made sure to invite runners who claimed Irish, English,

Native American, and Scottish ancestry. The English assumed they were superior in mind and body, and they were frequently at pains to prove it. Of an 1844 race featuring an assortment of nationalities and racial strains, Benjamin G. Rader noted that "It was the trial of the Indian against the white man, on the point in which the red man boasts his superiority. It was the trial of the peculiar American physique against the long-held supremacy of the English muscular endurance."[4] But after the Civil War, running became a true sport with specialized training and exacting demands. Within half a century the black man literally ran away with the records in running and jumping.

Athletics Becomes Organized

Just as boxing became distinct from barroom brawls and football evolved from wild, undisciplined team sport, so track— or "athletics," as it is called in the rest of the world—emerged from casual racing. Oxford and Cambridge Universities in England held their first dual meet in 1864, an event so well received that the British Empire Games were held two years later. Britain's dominions were worldwide in the mid-1800s, and they wanted athletic events to show off the finest British subjects. What better way to do that than by staging some games to see who could go the fastest, and farthest, with most endurance.

Here in America the New York Athletic Club (NYAC) was organized in 1866. It promoted its first meet in 1871. No blacks or other "disdained" ethnics belonged to the NYAC or other groups with "elite" membership, although everyone seemed interested in the posted results of contests. After all, runners required only a pair of shoes, and anyone with a watch could time the distances. The assumption was made by some that unless a runner belonged to one of these clubs, neither his efforts nor his times were to be taken seriously: "a superior athlete, unless he be black, a recent immigrant, or too crude in social demeanor, could expect little difficulty in finding a club that would grant him membership."[5]

Pedestrianism was dead by 1880. The inaugural intercollegiate meet was held in 1873, and the first National Amateur Track event was sponsored by the NYAC in 1876. The races in this first "national" affair included the 100-yard dash, the 120-yard high hurdles, the one-mile run, the three-mile run, and the seven-mile walk. These runs became the standard, pivotal events of all meets thereafter for a quarter-century. Notice that of the five races, three are distance runs. Endurance was then thought to be more important than short-distance speed.

The Amateur Athletic Union (AAU) was formed in 1888. It, too, reserved membership for young men of high social standing who fit the phrase "gentleman player." There was an opening of sorts on April 21, 1895, when the Penn Relay Carnival in Philadelphia began. It allowed anyone who was qualified to run in the team-oriented relays.

Denied admittance to national meets before 1895, blacks had to content themselves with their own arrangements, sponsored by groups like the Odd Fellows and colleges. Black institutions in the South

held "Special Days" when intramural activities were contested. To be sure, equipment was crude and facilities were substandard, but the attempt was made nevertheless. Academics were more pressing than athletics.

Early Black College and Public School Programs

Most black colleges stressed physical training early in their history. But Tuskegee Institute (now Tuskegee University) went a step further in 1890 when it hired James B. Washington, the school's bookkeeper, as its first sports director. Washington had learned the basics of baseball and running while at Hampton Institute (now Hampton University). Three years later in 1893, Tuskegee staged the first major black college track meet, using members of its military cadet battalions.

The events included—other than close-order drill—running, jumping, relays, weight throwing, broad jumping, wall scaling, standing broad jumping, tug-of-war, and a centipede race. There was no aping the format of the NYAC or AAU meets. The relays were deemed especially important in fostering teamwork, dedicated coordination of athletes, and persistence. Blacks were doubly damned at the time because northerners believed *all* southerners—black and white—were lazy, and said so. Caspar Whitney, Walter Camp's collaborator in the All-America football selections, said in *Harper's Weekly* magazine that "The Southerner is prone to 'drifting', and by the pleasantest route.... The athletic wave that has swept over the South has put new spirit into the young men, and lessened the receipts of saloons to an appreciable degree."[6]

Most sports administrators used manuals prepared by the YMCA and the A.G. Spaulding Company that laid out the requirements for facilities and training techniques. The most important contribution, however, came from black athletes who had returned from varsity participation in white schools up North. Most of these students received their admittance slips precisely because they showed promise in some sport. Some black institutions thus served as part of a "farm system" for certain white colleges.

Around the turn of the century, a black student from the South had to be a graduate of a black college before entering a white school as a freshman. It is not surprising, therefore, that a handful of white colleges had a long history of black participation while others had none at all. The idea that athletic talent could earn a place in a prestigious northern school was well grounded by the 1890s.

Matthew Bullock was a good example of this phenomenon. He was a star at Dartmouth and then organized the first intercollegiate track meet in 1907 for black colleges in the Southeast. From his base at Atlanta Baptist College (now Morehouse) he combined the best features of the Olympics and the Ivy League meets and the peculiarities of the triple-departmentalized black schools to field a successful event.

A year before Bullock's efforts in Atlanta, Harvard-trained Edwin B. Henderson sponsored the first intercity meet for black schoolboys in Washington, D.C., on May 30, 1906. Under the auspices of the Interscholastic Athletic Association (ISAA), nearly a hundred men and boys competed from the following schools: Howard University; the Washington, D.C., Colored YMCA; the "M" Street High School (now Dunbar); Armstrong Technical High School; Baltimore High School; and Wilmington (Delaware) High. It was a resounding success.

Blacks seemed to have found a formula that was enunciated by Colston R. Stewart a half a century later in the December 1951 *Negro History Bulletin*: "first, organized sport sifted down from the colleges and schools to the public; second, Negroes migrating North and entering public schools...; third, weaving their way onto track teams and community play associations...; fourth, there were more schools in the South for Negroes with athletic facilities...; and fifth, the Penn Relays Carnival began."

Strangely, some disinterest set in just before World War I. Poor facilities, uneven coaching, and competition from baseball in the spring made college track programs unappealing for a time. In the 1913 *ISAA Handbook*, Virginia Union University reported that "Track work has received little or no attention." However, the Colored (now Central) Intercollegiate Athletic Association (CIAA) was formed in 1912; it began to provide the organizational framework to advance the sport's cause after World War I.

Public school track programs had an interesting beginning. The precedent was set at Eton, the English secondary school for its upper class, in the early 1800s. The typical black public school in the South before 1900 was a one-room, dilapidated frame building. The best situation was a school connected with a black college that typically had a preparatory section included. Northern blacks had it a bit better, but unless the school system was integrated, the facilities were vastly inferior. One solution was the Public Schools Athletic League (PSAL).

The PSAL began in New York City to help occupy the city's youth in useful activities. Blacks took part immediately, and the ISAA encouraged its members to participate. The Smart Set Club, an organization formed in Brooklyn, New York, was so encouraged by the PSAL movement that it staged the first large indoor meet ever organized by blacks. Held on March 31, 1910, in Brooklyn's 14th Regiment Armory, the meet attracted over twenty-five hundred participants. Smart Set's reputation was further enhanced since it was the only black club allowed to enter relay teams in national AAU meets, though the club itself was not an AAU-affiliated organization.

The PSAL divided boys in track, swimming, and skating into four weight classes: midget, or less than 80 pounds; lightweight, or less than 95 pounds; middleweight, or less than 115 pounds; and unlimited. Girls had their own set of events: short-distance dashes, baseball throws, and short-distance swimming.

Black clubs in New York City in 1910 banded together to form the Vulcan Athletic League (VAL) to stage events in basketball, football, baseball, and track. Thus, on the eve of World War I black schoolboys—and some girls—had the ISAA, PSAL, the VAL, the Colored YMCAs, and the Sears, Roebuck–sponsored meets in Chicago to assist them in track activities. Later still, the

Police Athletic Leagues (PALs) started programs. The clubs had been encouraged by the successes of other blacks at white colleges, and in the Olympics and even those in other sports, like world champion cyclist Marshall Taylor.

Fortunately, Edwin B. Henderson recorded the best times and distances of blacks. He included them in the 1913 *ISAA Handbook*. Not including blacks who starred on varsity squads at white colleges, he listed the following results—which may look very surprising in the 1980s:[7]

100-yard dash	10.2 seconds
440-yard run	54.2 seconds
1-mile run	5.25 minutes
220-yard hurdles	27 seconds
12-pound hammer	121 feet
220-yard dash	23.6 seconds
880-yard run	2 min. 15.6 sec.
120-yard hurdles	18.6 seconds
12-pound shot	40' 3½"
High Jump	5' 8"
Broad Jump	21' 7"
Discus Throw	81' 3"
Pole Vault	9' 6"
2-mile run	11 min. 47 sec.

Stars at White Colleges

America's white colleges began track competition as an adjunct to rowing races in 1873. In 1852 James Gordon Bennett, a wealthy sportsman, had invited crew teams from Harvard and Yale to come to Lake Winnepesaukee in New York to race for his hotel guests. He added a two-mile run. The race proved so popular that other intercollegiate meets were soon arranged with the help of elite clubs in the Northeast.

Black America's first track star, William Tecumseh Sherman Jackson, emerged from this marriage of club and college. He attended Amherst College in Massachusetts from 1890 to 1892. There he played football with the first black All-America selectee, William Henry Lewis. Jackson received his early running experience at Virginia Normal and Industrial Institute (now Virginia State University), where he excelled at the half-mile run.

While at Amherst he set a school record of 2 minutes 5.4 seconds for the 880-yard run, and drew raves from critics. Said the *Worcester* (Massachusetts) *Telegram* on May 29, 1980, of one of his dual meets, "In it were an even dozen flyers.... But it remained for a new man to carry off the honors...W.T.S. Jackson, Amherst....The last is a Negro and an athlete of speed and stamina....Jackson forged ahead, winning in the remarkable time of 2:08.2. Considering the track and the wind it was one of the biggest efforts of the day."

At the time blacks were not perceived as being naturally fast or enduring on the tracks, since most neither had the benefit of training nor were allowed to participate in meets sponsored by the elite clubs. Jackson's performance, however, set some to thinking about the supposed "natural" advantages of his race.

The next star performer was Napoleon Bonaparte Marshall of Harvard, who ran from 1895 to 1897. His specialty was the quarter-mile. Marshall was born of well-to-do parents in Washington, D.C., on July 30, 1873, and had attended the well-heeled Phillips Andover Preparatory School before enrolling at Harvard. His best time for the 440-yard dash was 51.2, which he set as a

sophomore. The record at the time was 49.6, set by Thomas E. Burke of Boston University.

Two other pre-1900 names were Spencer Dickerson, a quarter-miler at the University of Chicago in 1896–97, and G.C.H. Burleigh at the University of Illinois, who scored a 16.6-second time for the 120-yard high hurdles. Most observers today would assume that blacks excelled at shorter dashes in the beginning since that is their forte at present. But nearly every noted performer on the cinder paths until 1910 was a distance specialist. In the 1890s endurance was more highly prized than sheer speed over a hundred yards—for people as well as for horses.

The first black champion on the track was Philadelphia-born John Baxter "Doc" Taylor, who attended the University of Pennsylvania in 1904 and 1907–1980. (He mysteriously left for the years 1905–06.) He went to racially mixed Central High School and Brown Preparatory before college. In 1904, wasting no time, he broke the Intercollegiate Amateur Athletic Association of America (ICAAAA) 440-yard-dash mark with a new time of 49.2 seconds. He repeated as ICAAAA victor in 1907 and 1908. He was coached part-time by the then dean of track coaches, Michael C. Murphy, who was an Olympic instructor in 1912.

On May 30, 1907, Taylor set a new mark of 48.8 in the ICAAAA Championships and was joined on the Penn squad by two other blacks—Howard Smith and Dewey Rogers, both half-milers. At the 1908 Olympic Games in London, Taylor was involved in a contretemps during a 400-meter race. There were severe disagreements between the American and British teams, and officials ordered the 400-meter finals rerun when they claimed that Taylor's teammate, J. C. Carpenter, deliberately ran wide and in front of Lieutenant Wyndham Halswelle, the British favorite, near the finish line.

The British, who had stationed officials around the track at twenty-yard intervals, cried "Foul!" and removed the tape at the finish line before the race was finished. Taylor was physically pulled off the track just before a half-hour argument between the Americans and the British. Carpenter was disqualified, and the race was ordered rerun with strings to divide the lanes. Taylor and his other teammate, W. C. Robbins, refused to cooperate. Halswelle ran the race alone and won the Gold Medal. Taylor did run the third leg on a first-place effort in the 4-by-400-meter medley relay in a combined time of 3:29.4 minutes. It was the first gold medal performance by a black American in Olympic history. The other black participant at London, W. C. Holmes, did not place in the standing broad jump.

Taylor returned to Philadelphia a hero and made plans to open a veterinary medical practice; but he suddenly died of typhoid pneumonia on December 2, 1908. He was only twenty-six.

Taylor's immediate predecessor in the Olympics was George Poage, who competed in 1904 at St. Louis, representing the Milwaukee Athletic Club. Poage won a bronze medal in the 400-meter hurdles, which featured four Americans from first to fourth place. (The winner, Harry Hillman, was a bank teller who never attended college and who advised swallowing whole raw eggs to enhance one's stomach and wind.) In the 400-meter run, Poage placed sixth. He ran the 100-yard dash, the 200-yard dash, the 220-yard hurdles, and the 440-yard dash at the University of Wisconsin. John B. Taylor broke Poage's collegiate record of forty nine seconds in the 440-yard dash in 1907.

One year after Taylor's performance in London, black America's first star in field events entered Harvard. He was Theodore "Ted" Cable, a five-foot-nine-inch, 185-pounder from Indianapolis, Indiana. Born in 1891, he graduated from Shortridge High School in his hometown and enrolled at Phillips Andover Academy. At Harvard he had not planned to do any sports activities, but he answered coach Pat Quinn's call for freshmen in the weight events. He wound up a team member in the 220-yard dash, the hammer throw, and the broad jump.

In the 1912 Harvard-Yale meet, Cable won the hammer throw with a heave of 154' 11¼", the first black to do so in a field event. He topped that off with a victory in the broad jump of 22' 10¼". At the Intercollegiate finals on May 18 at Cambridge, Massachusetts, he won the hammer throw, thus becoming its first black winner, too. He missed out on an Olympic berth that year, finishing third in the hammer throw trials and fourth in the hop, skip, and jump event. He repeated as Intercollegiate hammer-throw champion in 1913 at 162' 4½" and placed second at the AAU in the thirty-nine-pound weight throw. Alexander Louis Jackson joined Cable at Harvard in 1913 as a hurdler. From Englewood, New Jersey, Jackson first ran in meets sponsored by the Vulcan Athletic League. Those early pioneering efforts had begun paying dividends.

No one, though, was ready for Howard Porter Drew of Lexington, Virginia. He was the first in a continuing line of blacks known as "the world's fastest humans." Drew was born on June 28, 1890, and entered high school in Springfield, Massachusetts, at age twenty-one after working at a railroad depot. In 1910 this speedster won the National Junior 100-yard and 220-yard dash titles in 10 and 21.8 seconds, respectively. He repeated these victories in 1911. But 1912 was his banner year.

The 5′ 9″ Drew defeated the favored Ralph Craig of the University of Michigan in the Olympic Trials on June 8 in a time of 10.8 seconds for 100 meters. That equaled the existing Olympic record. But when he got to Stockholm for the Games, he pulled up lame after qualifying in his heat, and he could not run in the final. Nevertheless he recovered, and on November 11 of that year he lowered the 100-meter record to 10.2 seconds at an indoor meet at the 23rd Regiment Armory in Brooklyn.

On September 12 he captured the AAU 100-yard dash, finishing a full yard ahead of A. T. Myer. Then he equaled the American record in the 70-yard dash at 7.5 seconds and later broke it on December 7 with a clocking of 7.2 seconds. Reporters who were used to blacks doing well in distance races were perplexed by Drew's showing, since he seldom trained. Some say he injured himself in Stockholm precisely because he was forced to train as an American team member. The *New York Tribune* writer said, "It seems incredible that a man without fear of life and not the slightest desire to catch a train can impel himself to such prodigious speed."[8]

From the American coach, Mike Murphy, came the comment that "Never in my life have I seen any sprinter with such wonderful leg action…why, his legs fly back and forth just like pistons….Trainers and experts say that he has the quickest start of any man ever seen upon the track."[9]

In 1913 Drew again won the AAU titles in the 100-yard and 220-yard dashes, holding the world record in the latter at 22.8 seconds. But that most coveted of speed marks—the 100-yard dash—was equaled by him on September 1 at Charter Oak Park in Hartford, Connecticut. He sped the distance in 9.6 seconds, to write his name alongside Arthur Duffey's from 1902. He decided to enter the University of Southern California, and in 1914 he was a co-holder of the 220-yard dash record at 21.2 seconds.

Unfortunately, there were no Olympics in 1916 because of World War I, so after switching to and graduating from Drake University, he entered the Army and prepared for the Inter-Allied Games in Paris in 1919. He failed to qualify for the 1920 Olympics but was named to an All-America list of track stars in 1918, which represented the best of all time. Alan J. Gould, the Associated Press sports editor, said it for everyone: "Drew was the greatest of them all."[10] Drew and Andy Ward, the AAU winner in the 100-meter and 200-meter, could have done well in an Olympics in 1916.

A contemporary of Howard P. Drew was another world record holder, Henry Binga Dismond of Richmond, Virginia. After surpassing the quarter-mile competition at home, he went to Howard University and then to the University of Chicago, where he was tutored by Amos Alonzo Stagg. In 1913 he ran a 47.8-second time for 440 yards and was hailed as the second coming of John B. Taylor. Two years later he managed to equal the world record held by

Ted Meredith at 47.4. Between seasons he competed for the Smart Set Club and the Loughlin Lyceum.

Other quarter-milers included Cecil Lewis at the University of Chicago; James E. Meredith at Penn; and Irving T. Howe of Boston's English High School and later of Dartmouth and Colby College. W. Randolph Granger, of Barringer High School in Newark, New Jersey, ran the half-mile at Dartmouth; J. Ferguson was a two-miler at Ohio State via West Virginia Institute (now West Virginia State); Howard Martin ran at the University of Cincinnati; Jim Ravenelle was a quarter-miler at NYU; Ben Johnson competed in dashes at Springfield (Massachusetts); Fred "Duke" Slater tossed the shot put at Iowa; and football giant Paul Robeson threw the weights at Rutgers.

Edward Solomon Butler was an exception. He was the first African-American to star abroad in more than one event. John B. Taylor had earned glory in the London Olympics for his specialty, but Butler could do everything. He hailed from Wichita, Kansas, where he was born in 1895. His family had been part of the large migration of blacks to Kansas in 1879. Beginning at Hutchinson High School, he followed his coach to Rock Island (Illinois) High School and flourished.

At a scholastic meet there, Butler won all five events he entered: the 100-yard, the 220-yard, the 440-yard, the high jump, and the broad jump titles. Illinois officials thereafter passed a rule then limiting entrants to two events. He also played football and basketball. Entering Dubuque (Iowa) University in 1915, he immediately set records that stood until the depression. Noted the *Des Moines Register* of December 13, 1915,

"Butler is the fastest man who ever set foot on Hawkeye soil."

After graduation he found himself in the Inter-Allied Games in 1919, where he made the third-longest long jump in history—24' 9½", only 2¼" behind the world record. He returned to America with five medals and two diplomas after the King of Montenegro presented his awards to him.

Black runners had come quite a distance since W.T.S. Jackson began at Amherst. They began at the middle-distance events and ended World War I with a reputation for all-around swiftness.

Military Successes

Black soldiers gained much acclaim in the Army. Before 1900 only a handful had had any formal training, but they had made good showings at military meets. In 1908 black military units won the track team titles in all three Philippine Department contests. The 9th Cavalry won the Luzon meet over the white 3rd Cavalry, 10th Cavalry (Black), 5th Field Artillery, and 26th, 29th, and 30th Infantries. The 24th Infantry won the Visayas meet, and the 25th Infantry captured the Mindanao events.

The following year, Private George Washington of the 25th Infantry won the 100-yard, 220-yard, and 880-yard events in the Philippines Championships. On February 26, 1916, a Private Gilbert (no first name could be found) equaled the world mark in the 100-yard dash at 9.6 seconds in Honolulu. Sergeant Schley C. Williamson was easily the Army's fastest soldier from 1917 through 1920, clocking 9.8 seconds for 100 yards. As in football and basketball, black soldiers took tremendous pride in their athletic accomplishments. With superior facilities and a high level of general fitness, they were always ready to race.

By 1920 the black runner was an enigma to most experts. The white man still theorized that *he* was physically and mentally superior. Jack Johnson, the black former heavyweight champion, had lost his title, and no black heavyweights were given a chance for another seventeen years. What began as ideas about black musculature to explain why they were distance runners soon had to be altered to account for Howard P. Drew and Private Gilbert. In fact, white theorists had to invert their racist notions completely for a time. Beginning with Drew and Butler, black athletes dominated the dash and jumping events. Before World War II closed another chapter in the saga of track and field, several more blacks made the timers check their watches in disbelief, especially one named James Cleveland "Jesse" Owens.

Notes

1. *Horizon History of Africa,* vol. 1, p. 184.
2. David K. Wiggins, "The Play of Slave Children in the Plantation Communities of the Old South, 1820–1860." *Journal of Sports History* 7(Summer 1980): 32.
3. Frederick Douglass, op. cit., p. 145.
4. Rader, op. cit., p. 40.
5. Rader, op. cit., p. 60.
6. Somers, op. cit., p. 246.
7. *ISAA Handbook* (1913), p. 123.
8. Quoted in Henderson, *The Negro in Sport.* (1949), p. 50.
9. Quoted in ibid., p. 51.
10. Alan J. Gould, The Associated Press, April 5, 1928.

CHAPTER 2

1918–1945

Herculean strides were made between the two World Wars by black track and field athletes. Most of the gains came in the 1930s and early 1940s, as contrasted with the slow pace of progress in the 1920s. The talent was overwhelmingly concentrated in white college varsity teams and in clubs that were formed for this very purpose. Black colleges were woefully unable to offer anything resembling a track program until well into the 1930s. They had squads but their results were not very substantial.

Black schools struggled just to meet their academic demands, which increased considerably after the First World War. In addition, track suffered the same fate as basketball since it fell within the tourist season down South, where all but five black colleges were located. Baseball was the primary spring sport and it was buttressed by a traditional Easter Monday game, which usually attracted several hundred former alumni to campus for reunions and other festivities.

Track and field facilities were lacking, coaching was rudimentary, conference competition did not begin until 1924, with the Colored Intercollegiate Athletic Association (CIAA) meet, and there were no role models to follow. Football and baseball were the most important activities and every other sport was secondary. The track programs at the segregated public high schools in the South were present in name only—if present at all. Typically, blacks were not expected to go to school after the seventh grade. Nearly everyone was engaged in farming or its subsidiary businesses. In short, track was just not very important.

Black clubs in the northern cities with access to quality competition fared well. Some had a long history of performers dating back to the early 1900s and many of their members wound up in prestigious white schools. None of these clubs belonged to the Amateur Athletic Union (AAU) until the mid-1920s, but informal arrangements with meet organizers were usually enough to gain admission for a select number of competitors. Few blacks had the time or the inclination to train for a sport that offered no professional outlet. The usual work week was six days and time off meant money lost.

At some white colleges, black athletes were able to gain worldwide attention. Competition began in dual meets with other schools and was augmented—for the very best—by conference meets, Intercollegiate Amateur Athletic Association of America (ICAAAA) meets, National Collegiate Athletic Association (NCAA) meets, AAU meets, special invitational meets, and the Olympic Games, which never saw a product from a black college until after the Second World War.

Facilities at white schools were state-of-the-art and supplemented by government funds in some instances, as when the Reserve Officers Training Corps (ROTC) was established and monies were provided for drill fields. Black colleges never saw a dime of these appropriated stipends. Another prime source of support came from wealthy alumni who donated, bequeathed, or just built athletic facilities for their alma mater. What with all these advantages and a willingness born of long-standing tradition, it is no wonder that black America's most illustrious track and field athletes matriculated at these institutions.

It would have been foolhardy to go on record in 1919 and predict that, within a quarter of a century, blacks would hold nearly all the world sprinting and jumping records. But that is exactly what happened in spite of their having to suffer the most vicious form of institutionalized racism which went undirected at their less athletically gifted brethren.

Black College Track

Within three years of the end of the First World War, the sport of track took giant organizational strides to meet the growing demand for quality competition. Of all the major sports played in America, track was the most universally known and the easiest to arrange. It was the centerpiece of the Olympics and a victorious America was eager to maintain her preeminence.

The YMCA staged its first national meet in 1920; the Olympics resumed in 1920 after an eight-year hiatus because of World War I (though Germany, Austria, Hungary, Turkey, and Russia were not invited); the NCAA began its meets in 1921; and the CIAA finally held its inaugural meet in 1924. But black college track programs were, in most instances, nonexistent. Only Hampton Institute (now Hampton University) could claim more than elementary expertise. Their dominance was such that only Lincoln University (Pennsylvania) and Morgan State won CIAA titles between 1924 and 1931. The Southern Intercollegiate Athletic Conference (SIAC) began track in 1916 and then discontinued it until 1938. Southern, segregated white colleges were not that interested in track either. Less than a half a dozen of them placed their stars on the Olympic teams before 1932. As at black colleges, only football and baseball mattered.

Howard University won that first CIAA meet and a sample of the winning times and distances makes interesting reading today. The results were: 100-yard dash = 10.2 seconds; 440-yard dash = 53 seconds; long jump = 20' 10"; pole vault = 9' 3"; high jump = 5' 6". It is important to avoid drawing the wrong inferences from these results. In the 1920s, black colleges were bastions of privilege for a small number of students in three separate departments: grade school, preparatory department, and the college-level department. In 1924, there was simply no history of track superiority to emulate.

It was 1927 before any black land grant schools—the state-supported institutions—received their accreditation and that was bestowed by the *northern* branch of the Association of Colleges and Secondary

Schools. The southern branch would not dare accredit black schools for fear their graduates would press for jobs reserved for whites. The one major, prestigious competition that would accept blacks was the Penn Relays at Franklin Field in Philadelphia. In 1923, Lincoln University won the one-mile relay there.

As if to reinforce the egalitarian code of this competition, Dr. George Overton, the Penn Relays director in the 1920s, mentioned to the *Chicago Defender* reporter William White that he would see to it that racial discrimination would not be a factor. Furthermore, he added that black colleges were backward in athletics but that, in track at least, they could develop performers like John B. Taylor and Howard Porter Drew. One particularly bright result was George D. Williams of Hampton Institute, who in 1930 placed second in the javelin and a year later set a meet record of 197' 1½".

Tuskegee copied the format of the Penn Relays and began its own Relay Carnival on May 7, 1927; the first by a black college. The May 14 *New York Age* printed this account of Tuskegee athletic director Cleveland Abbott's success: "...Tuskegee's entire student body with a large number of visitors from Columbus [Georgia], Montgomery, Atlanta and other points were on hand to witness a thorough and comprehensive demonstration of the possibilities of the youth of our race."[1] It is worth noting that a northern black newspaper like the *New York Age* thought enough of the Carnival's potential to provide wide coverage for the event.

When Abbott began his school's Relay Carnival, there were no events for women at the Penn Relays, but he did not forget them.

He inserted two events that first year: the 100-yard dash and a 440-yard relay. In 1930, he added the 50-yard dash and the discus. None of the CIAA schools had varsity competition for women at the time, so he broke new ground against establishment opposition.

In 1917 in France, a Women's Sports Federation was formed, and four years later the Women's International Sports Federation was organized to minister to women's athletics and to formulate policy. In 1922 the first Olympics for women were held in Paris, that led to their inclusion at regularly scheduled Olympiads beginning in 1928. In 1924, the AAU staged its first national championships for women. In 1926, Gertrude Ederle, white, swam the English Channel in fourteen hours and twenty-three minutes and broke the men's record by two hours. That same year at Lincoln Park in Chicago, Viola Edwards set a new AAU record in the high jump at 5' ⅛", surpassing the old mark of 4' 9". All of these developments led Abbott to believe that women should not be ignored.

But Abbott's foresight was not shared by everyone. Most black women spent very little time engaged in competitive, organized sport. They worked in the home with few appliances of convenience. There were no washers and dryers, no dishwashers, no disposable diapers, and the average work day was twelve hours long. In the South, two-thirds of all black women who worked outside their own homes did so as domestics in the homes of whites. The only times for recreation were Saturday and Sunday afternoons. The percentage of black college women heavily involved in sport was probably less than 5 percent.

As late as 1930, one black paper, the *California Eagle,* reported on March 14 that "Colored girls are showing a smaller percentage engaged in regular athletic sports than any other race in the Los Angeles area....In this wonderful climate, where outdoor sports may be played year-round, and there's no color bar set up at the gym door or the playgrounds, is there any reason why our girls have fallen so far behind our boys?"[2] The answer was yes, they had work to do and society considered track to be a masculine endeavor. Inez Patterson of Temple University was the outstanding exception to this trend.

In the 1930s, two more black college conferences began track competition—the Midwestern Athletic Association (MWAA), in 1933, and the Southwestern Athletic Conference (SWAC), in 1939. Wilberforce University won all save one of the MWAA titles through the decade, but in 1937 there was no conference meet at all. The SWAC's focus was football until well into the 1940s—football was the *only* conference title awarded until 1939, when basketball and track were added. Normal black occupational routines were to go to school through the sixth or seventh grade if possible, and then get a job wherever someone could pull some strings. Willie Mays, perhaps the most versatile baseball player ever, almost went to work in a saw mill because his father was there.

Consequently, by the end of the decade, southern black track aspirants had only three major meets in which to perform: the Penn Relays, the CIAA meet, and a new Tuskegee Carnival. Anything of significance was likely to come out of one of these events and that is exactly what happened. Abbott paid increasing attention to his female students and the results were positive. He felt encouraged enough to enter a team in the 1936 AAU Nationals, and their second place finish was the highest yet attained by a black school in any AAU National meet.

When Abbott came to Tuskegee in the mid-1920s he did so in the aftermath of a devastating resolution passed by the Council on Women's Sports in 1923. Through ignorance, custom, and chauvinism, the council resolved to urge women's sports organizations to deemphasize keen competition. Abbott thought the advice was too strong and proceeded to build a powerhouse track team—the best by any black college until World War II. He even hired a female, Amelia C. Roberts, as the team's coach. In 1937, the team won the AAU Nationals and began the black female domination of some events that exists in America today.

In that first championship season, the team amassed thirty-three points at Trenton, New Jersey, and the star was Lula Mae Hymes who competed and scored in the 100 meters, the long jump, and the 400-meter relay. Tuskegee even had a second team entered. The members of that winning squad were Hymes, Cora Gaines in the hurdles, Florence Wright in the shotput, Lelia Perry in the long jump, Mable Smith and Esther Brown in the sprints, Margaret Barnes in the javelin, Melissa Fitzpatrick in the baseball throw, and the relay team of Hymes, Brown, Jessie Abbott (Cleveland Abbott's daughter), and Celestine Birge. The coach was Christine Evans Petty who had replaced Miss Roberts. Here are their times and distances.

- 80-meter hurdles .... 1st place
  Cora Gaines .... 12.8 seconds
- long jump .... 1st place
  Lula Hymes .... 17′ 8½″
- 50-meter dash .... 2nd place
  Lula Hymes .... 6.8 seconds
- high jump .... 2nd place
  Cora Gaines .... 4′ 10½″
- 400-meter relay .... 2nd place
  Birge, Abbott, Smith, Hymes 51 seconds
- shotput .... 2nd place
  F. Wright .... 37′ 5″
- discus .... 2nd place
  F. Wright .... 105′ 1″
- baseball throw .... 2nd place
  M. Fitzpatrick .... 229′ 5″
- 100 meters .... 4th place
  Jessie Abbott .... 12.8 seconds
- 200-meter dash .... 4th place
  Mable Smith .... 27 seconds

In the previous AAU meet in 1936, Mable Smith set a new American citizenship record in the long jump at eighteen feet. Smith and her teammates would have never received this kind of attention in a white college track program. Most of the female AAU participants came not from universities but from clubs. White college varsity sports for women in the 1930s followed the 1923 Women's Sports Council resolutions to the letter. Their roughest activity was probably field hockey.

It might be expected that Tuskegee's main competition would come from another black school but it in fact came from northern clubs, especially the Mercury Athletic Club in New York City and the Illinois Women's Athletic Club. Two Mercury stalwarts were Gertrude Johnson and Ivy Wilson. Johnson was the AAU 200 meters winner in 1937 and the 50 meters winner in

1939. At another AAU sanctioned meet, Johnson became the first contestant to enter and score in five events: the 50-yard dash, the 100-yard dash, the 220-yard dash, the baseball throw, and the long jump. Wilson won the 50 meters title in 1936. Other members of that Mercury team included Ida Byrne, Pearl Edwards, Romona Harris, Etta Tate, and Esther Dennis. Mercury won the 1937 AAU 400-meter relay event and a year later they annexed the Canadian National Outdoor title under coach Leroy Alston.

Tuskegee's women speedsters continued their winning ways through the eve of the 1948 Olympics in London. They repeated as team victors in 1938 through 1942 and won the inaugural AAU Indoor title in 1941. In 1943, the Cleveland Polish team, led by Stella Walsh, captured the honors but Tuskegee returned to form in 1944 through 1948. Alice Coachman assumed the leadership role from Hymes in 1942 by contending for the sprints and the high jump. She won the AAU Outdoor 50-meter title four times, the 100 meters three times, and the high jump title an incredible nine times. Indoors, she won the 50-meter title twice, and the high jump three times. At five feet eight inches, this Albany, Georgia, native had first attracted attention as a seventh-grader when she vaulted 5′ 4½″, less than an inch from the world mark. Keep in mind that in this era the jumpers took off with both feet flying rather than taking off with one foot as today. Coachman literally *owned* the high jump for a decade.

Rounding out the Tuskegee teams of the war years, the featured student-athletes were Lillie Purifoy, a three-time AAU 80-meter hurdles winner and long jump victor;

Lucy Newell, a 50-meter dash winner; Juanita Watson, a 50-meter and 100-meter winner; and the incomparable Hattie Turner, black America's first superlative performer in the discus and the baseball throw.

Tuskegee's one major black college competitor was Wilberforce, which was in the MWAA conference. That institution's Betty Jean Lane won the AAU Outdoor 50-meter title in 1940, the 100-meter title in 1940-41, and the 200-meter title in 1941. Indoors, she captured the 50-meter and 100-meter crowns in 1941. The only other groups to show consistently good results in this period were the West Philadelphia Athletic Club and the Harrisburg (Pennsylvania) Athletic Association. If it had not been for the black college, track for black women in the South would have been non-existent.

The mantle began to pass to another black school in 1944, when Jessie Abbott left her father's school to become track coach at Tennessee A&I (now Tennessee State). Walter Davis of Tennessee A&I was convinced that Cleveland Abbott's program could be cloned and he meant to try. "Good physical training...and good discipline would be good for the girls rather than harmful....We knew that there was nothing to prove that competitive sports was harmful. And we decided to go into it....We had seen Abbott win the AAU with Negro girls, and being a geneticist I know that individuals are born equal...and it's the environment that makes the difference."[3] Tennessee State dominated women's track in the 1950s.

While black women garnered most of the publicity at black schools, there were a few men who made the headlines. After

George Williams' high jump performances in 1932, Lloyd Thompson of Xavier University (New Orleans) followed him with an AAU victory in 1937 at 6' 6". Two years later, John Borican of Virginia State College (now Virginia State University) smashed several distance marks. He was American record holder at 600 yards (1 minute 10.2 seconds in 1941), 880 yards (1 minute 50.5 seconds in 1940), 800 meters (1 minute 50 seconds in 1942), and the AAU pentathlon winner in 1938, 1939, and 1941. He was the most talented all-around black performer between 1936 and 1942.

Lilburn Williams of Xavier was the AAU shotput winner in 1939. Mozelle Ellerbee of Tuskegee was the collegiate 100-yard dash champion in 1938 at 9.7 seconds and in 1939 at 9.8 seconds. Mel Walker of Tennessee State was high jump winner in 1941 at 6' 6½". Adam Berry of Southern University (Baton Rouge, Louisiana) leaped the same height—6' 6½"—in 1942. And Lewis Smith of Prairie View A&M was the AAU 600-yard indoor champion in 1943. He later attended Virginia Union. The only pole vault notable was Virginia Union's Howard Jones, who managed 13' 3" in 1936 with a wooden pole; fiberglass was not yet standard equipment.

By 1940, the South Central Athletic Conference (SCAC) began its competitions and joined the CIAA, SWAC, SIAC, and MWAA in trying to upgrade performances. Problems remained much as before: lack of adequate facilities, coaches like Morgan State's Eddie Hurt were overworked, fewer competitions, and the inability to secure certification for meet records in AAU standings. No American or world record set in a black college meet would have been accepted by the AAU or the ICAAAA. This fact alone was often reason enough for a promising black speedster to seek his education at a white school. It was little wonder then that white college results were looked upon as the times and distances to emulate.

Stars on White College Tracks

A berth on a major white college track team was nearly all any runner could want. The facilities were the best to be found, the competition was always keen, the coaching was at least adequate, and any records set were instantly certified. But as with other black students on white campuses, such problems as housing, jobs, and the limited use of university amenities were insulting but tolerated. After all, the alternative was either a black school or a club with AAU recognition. In most cases, if it were not for their athletic prowess, blacks would not be attending at all. However insulted, by the end of the Second World War, these token black athletes had rewritten the record books.

The big names just after the First World War were Fred "Duke" Slater, who starred in weight events at Iowa, and Edward Solomon Butler of Dubuque Seminary, who was a long jumper. Butler made the Olympic team in 1920, only to injure himself in his first leap in Antwerp, Belgium. But the most fuss was caused by two all-purpose athletes from the University of Michigan and Harvard: William DeHart Hubbard and Ned Gourdin.

Hubbard had attended Walnut Hills High School in Cincinnati, Ohio, and entered Michigan in 1921. He was an immediate sensation as a freshman in tying the

school record in the 50-yard dash, setting a freshman record in the long jump at 24' 6¾", winning the AAU long jump title at 24' 5½", winning the hop, step, and jump at 48' 1½", and being named an All-America. Michigan even lengthened the jumping pit just for him.

In his sophomore year, Hubbard set Big Ten marks in the 50-yard dash and the long jump at 25' 1½", and captured the hop, step, and jump again. In 1924, the Olympic year, he was Big Ten winner in the 100-yard dash at 9.8 seconds and the long jump. He might have been a threat on Michigan's football team but its coach, Fielding "Hurry Up" Yost, did not allow blacks on the team. At the Olympic Games in Paris, Hubbard captured a gold medal in the long jump— 24' 5⅛"—after qualifying on his second leap.

Still improving as a senior, he tied the 100-yard dash world record in a dual meet against Ohio State at 9.6 seconds, and later won the national title. His most illustrious feat, however, was a 25' 10⅞" long jump world mark on June 13, 1925, at Stagg Field in the NCAA championships. Hubbard's record was inspirational, noted the *California Eagle* in its June 26 edition, "...your blood tingled with pride and you shared with Michigan's greatest athlete his big triumph....We bow to King Hubbard, the persistent one."[4] A physical education major at school, he later took a position with the Cincinnati Recreation Department. When he graduated, Hubbard was one of only eight blacks in a class of 1,456.

One of Hubbard's Olympic teammates was Edward Orval "Ned" Gourdin of Jacksonville, Florida. Gourdin managed to graduate from Cambridge Latin Preparatory

School in Boston before entering Harvard. He was not planning to try out for track; he fancied himself a baseball player. But he certainly fooled everyone in 1921. In the Harvard–Yale meet he won the long jump at 24' 4"; the 100-yard dash in 10.4 seconds on a muddy track; and finished second in the 220-yard dash. Against Princeton—which did not admit blacks then—Gourdin won all three of the above events. His long jump performance set a new collegiate record at 24' 6". Said Princeton's coach, Keene Fitzpatrick, "There goes a whole track team and a man who ranks with [Alvin] Kraenzlein, who was the greatest all-around I ever saw in action."[5]

On July 23 at a Harvard–Yale and Oxford–Cambridge meet, Gourdin became the first to break the 25-foot barrier in a leap of 25' 3", which the August 21 *New York Telegram* said was a jump that "…was considered almost impossible.…We may begin to think of a day when the 26-footer will arrive…the achievement of Gourdin stands out, however, as the greatest feat in track and field in a generation."[6] Just to tease his opposition, on October 12, he captured the AAU Pentathlon at Travers Island, New York, by amassing twelve combined points in the long jump, javelin, 100-meter dash, discus, and 1500 meters. He repeated this pentathlon win in 1922 and won a silver medal in the 1924 Olympic long jump event.

Gus Moore hailed from Brooklyn's Boys High School and later the University of Pittsburgh. He was the fastest schoolboy miler ever—at 4 minutes 28.2 seconds—in 1925, only three-fifths of a second slower than the collegiate mark that year. In college, he broke R. Earl Johnson's six-mile cross country record in 27 minutes 32.6 seconds, while winning the title in 1928-29. He was AAU 10-mile champion in 1930.

The AAU National meet in 1927 set a precedent by relocating from New Orleans to Lincoln, Nebraska, because of possible racial discrimination. New Orleans meet officials just refused to accept black entrants so the venue was changed. Had this been football with more money at stake, the black performers would have merely been left at home. But some schools had little chance of winning without their black student-athletes. As the 1920s closed, blacks had distinguished themselves in the long jump and were about to serve notice in the sprints.

The black domination in the short races began with two Olympians in 1932, and put into overdrive with the most acclaimed athlete of the first half of this century. Thomas "Eddie" Tolan, Jr. and Ralph Metcalfe both came from the Midwest and were promising athletes as far back as high school. Tolan attended Detroit's Cass Technical High School and Metcalfe went to Chicago's Tilden Technical High. Tolan entered the University of Michigan and Metcalfe went to Marquette. Both wound up side-by-side at the 1932 Olympics in Los Angeles.

Tolan, at five feet six inches and 130 pounds, was the American schoolboy champion in the 100-yard and 220-yard dashes. He set a new world record in the 100-yard mark on May 25, 1929, at 9.5 seconds. Two weeks later, George Simpson, white, lowered the mark to 9.4 seconds using starting blocks which were disdained at first. (For a time, two separate sets of records were kept for dashes using blocks and for those set without them.) In 1930, Tolan was Big Ten champion Indoors for 60 yards in 6.2 seconds, the outdoor 100-yard winner at 9.6 seconds, and the 220-yard winner at 20.9 seconds. His black teammate, Booker Brooks, was Big Ten discus champion in 1930, with a heave of 142' 6" and second in the shotput at 46' 6⅜".

On July 1, 1930, Tolan set a new world record in the 100-meter dash at 10.2 seconds that included a win over Simpson and Percy Williams, the Olympic champion at that distance. That summer also proved to be a trying time for him. In September, Tolan, Gus Moore, and John Lewis were denied lodging at the Illinois Athletic Club and the Chicago Athletic Club where their teammates were staying for an AAU event against Great Britain. Threatening to leave, Tolan was told by an AAU official that he would "...be through in athletics forever..." if he quit the team.[7]

Tolan wired his mother for advice and was urged to run his heart out, though others advised him to leave. The three athletes eventually stayed at the Grand Hotel, a black inn on Chicago's South Side. Phil Edwards, the black British runner, stayed with his team members at the Medinah Athletic Club. Metcalfe, from Chicago originally, stayed at home. It was a classic case of suffering the indignity of racial rejection if he stayed, or of missing out on a solid accomplishment if he left. It would not be the last time it happened to them.

Metcalfe was born in Atlanta, Georgia, on May 29, 1910, and moved to Chicago with his family. At five feet eleven inches and 180 pounds, he had burst upon the scene in 1930 when, as a member of the Chase Athletic Club, he won the AAU Junior 100-yard dash title in 9.7 seconds. His big day came on June 11, 1932, when he shattered the world record in the 220-yard dash and tied Tolan's 100-yard dash mark at 9.5 seconds. But for both Metcalfe and Tolan, the supreme test was the 1932 Olympic Games in Los Angeles, where the city had raised $1.5 million in bonds to be added to state funds of another million to showcase America's first Olympics since 1904. The most awaited event was the 100-yard dash final with Tolan, Metcalfe, and Simpson at the starting line.

Metcalfe was favored but he false-started and was away last with the second shot of the starter's pistol. Tolan led at fifty meters and Metcalfe caught him at ninety meters but "The timer's clock, however, caught the Michigan marvel's chest a hair's breadth ahead of Metcalfe at the end."[8] Tolan's time was 10.3 seconds, a new Olympic and world record. He returned to capture the 200 meters as well in 21.2 seconds for another Olympic record. It was the first gold medal performance for a black American athlete in a sprint event. Michigan's Willis Ward said that "Tolan slackened near the finish enabling Metcalfe, the favorite, to win..." in the trials.[9] If Ward is correct, Tolan must have wanted Metcalfe to shoulder the pressure of being the favorite in the Games; in any case it worked.

Ed Gordon of the University of Iowa won the long jump gold medal at 25' ¾". He had collected the collegiate title earlier at 25' 3⅜". Other blacks who just missed making the United States team were discus thrower Booker Brooks of Michigan; high jumper Willis Ward of Michigan; Eugene Beatty, a hurdler from Michigan Normal (State); John Brooks, a long jumper; Ben

Eastman, a quarter-miler; and the javelin expert George Williams of Hampton Institute.

James Johnson of Illinois State Normal was a victim of an unfortunate turn of events. He was left off the 400-meter relay team after finishing fifth in the 100-meter dash trials. Past tradition had put the fifth and sixth place finishers in the 100-meter and the 200-meter finals on the 400-meter relay team, but at the last minute Johnson was replaced by Bob Kiesel and Hec Dyer with no explanation. Maybe the authorities meant to start a new tradition or just continue an old one of dispensing with blacks at will.

The two black women team members, Louise Stokes and Tydie Pickett, were members of the 400-meter relay but did not win a medal. Stokes ran for the Onteona Athletic Club in Malden, Massachusetts. She finished in a tie for fourth in the 100-meter dash trials while Pickett finished sixth in the 400-meter trials.

Those memorable 1932 Olympic Games were elementary compared to the 1936 Games in Berlin, Germany. More has been written about this Olympiad than about any other because of three facts: the German leader, Adolf Hitler, planned to demonstrate his theories of Aryan racial superiority through athletics; the undeniable talents of Jesse Owens, a black American sprinter and jumper; and reports of atrocities against Jews in Germany at the time. But the center of attention was Jesse Owens, who came upon his fame due to an unlikely set of circumstances.

Jesse Owens was named James Cleveland Owens after his birth on September 12, 1913, in Oakville, Alabama. One of twelve children of Henry and Emma Owens, Jesse was one of nine that survived. He did not grow up in good health, having suffered from bronchitis brought on from drafty winter winds and growths on his legs and chest that doctors could not decipher. Owens was not an especially good student, but he later acquired an ability to express himself quite well.

His family members were very religious, which may have helped him withstand the racial discrimination meted out to blacks in Alabama. Though Owens never had many unkind words to say about his early life there, another black Alabama sprinter contemporary, Eulace Peacock, lamented that "When I look back over my lifetime I can get so bitter about things that happened to me. And actually I should hate white people, but fortunately my family didn't bring me up that way."[10] Young Jesse must have had similar sentiments.

Owens' family moved to Cleveland, Ohio, in the early 1920s, and he again faced a new set of segregated movies and other recreational amenities. At the Bolton Elementary School, his teacher misunderstood Owens to say "Jesse" when asked his name rather than "J.C." in his slow, southern drawl. "Jesse" stuck. At Fairmont Junior High School, he met his future wife, Minnie Ruth Solomon, and discovered the joys of organized sports, mainly basketball and track. He also met his primary mentor and friend, Charles Riley, the school's coach and physical education teacher.

Riley, who was white and of average build—five feet eight inches—may have seen something of William DeHart Hubbard in Owens' speed, because he literally made his young protégé his life's work.

Owens even lunched at Riley's home, where Riley spared no efforts in making him faster. Within a year, Owens had clocked 11 seconds in the 100-yard dash and at age fifteen he set world marks for a junior high school student of 6' in the high jump and 22' 11¾" in the long jump. Riley even arranged for Owens to meet Hubbard, who had set the world record in the long jump in 1925.

In 1930 Owens was in East Technical High School, in a group of blacks that made up less than 5 percent of the students. In two years, he was the hottest track property in the country, bar none. He competed in the 1932 Midwest Olympic Preliminaries but lost in the long jump, the 100 meters, and the 200 meters. He became a father on August 8 when his daughter, Gloria, was born to Minnie Ruth. He then finished high school after setting a schoolboy record in the long jump of 24' 3¾". Later, at the National Interscholastic meet at Stagg Field in Chicago, Owens soared 24' 9⅝" in the long jump, tied the world mark in the 100-yard dash in 9.4 seconds, and set a new world record in the 220-yard dash in 20.7 seconds. Of East Tech's fifty-four total points, Owens accounted for thirty of them. He was even feted with a parade back in Cleveland. Strangely, not a single black college made an attempt to recruit him, so he wound up at Ohio State after seriously considering a few others.

But Ohio State had a sordid reputation among black Ohioans in the early 1930s. In 1931, William Bell, a black Ohio State football player, was benched in a game against Vanderbilt (Tennessee) that was played at *home*. In 1933, the Ohio State Supreme Court upheld the university's right to deny housing to a black co-ed, Doris Weaver,

because, as school president Dr. George Rightmire said, "Knowing the feelings in Ohio, can the administration take the burden of establishing this relationship—colored and white girls living in this more or less family way?"[11] Rightmire must have been talking about the feelings of white Ohioans.

The black press urged Owens to think twice before entering his choice of schools. "Why help advertise an institution that majors in prejudice?"[12] cried the *Chicago Defender*. Nevertheless, with his 73.5 high school grade-point-average, Owens enrolled in Ohio State in the fall of 1933. He had to share a boarding house apartment with some other black students because on-campus housing was barred to blacks. For him and his black friends, only one movie theater was accessible—upstairs, no university restaurants would admit them, and Owens himself was given the least visible job as a freight elevator operator in the State Office Building. The passenger elevator job was reserved for white athletes. Owens did not complain for he was paying his own way through college; he did not have a free ride as is the possibility today. (In those days, a scholarship was in fact a ready-made job for a student.) But 1933 was not all bad. John Brooks was Big Ten long jump champion at the University of Chicago; James Luvalle was ICAAAA winner in the 440-yard dash; and Eulace Peacock was the national pentathlon victor.

Problems aside, Owens' track potential seemed harnessed until the end of his sophomore season when he exploded with stellar performances on one Saturday afternoon. At the National Intercollegiates in Ann Arbor, Michigan, on May 25, 1935,

Owens put on a mind-boggling display that resulted in three world records and a tie in another. The new marks were a 20.3-second clocking in the 220-yard dash, a 22.6-second time in the 220-yard low hurdles, a leap of 26' 8¼" in the long jump, and a tied world mark in the 100-yard dash in 9.4 seconds. It was simply the most superlative feat ever accomplished in the history of the sport.

The black press was understandably effusive in praise. Said the June 8, 1935, *Norfolk* (Virginia) *Journal and Guide:* "Owens...is without doubt the greatest individual performer the world has ever known."[13] It also noted that coverage in the white daily papers in Birmingham and Atlanta was relegated to page three. Up North, the June 2, 1935, *New York Times* carried a banner headline, "Owens' Record-Breaking Feats Presage Brilliant Olympic Mark" and then reopened a discussion of why blacks make better runners. The *Times* added that "A theory has been advanced that through some physical characteristic of the race involving the bone and muscle construction of the foot and leg the Negro is ideally adapted to the sprints and jumping events."[14] Need more be said about this ridiculous notion that was thought to be just the reverse before Eddie Tolan and Ralph Metcalfe won the sprints at the 1932 Olympics? No matter what blacks did, white experts had to concoct a "theory" to explain it.

Owens' accomplishments overshadowed other outstanding performances by black stars. Willis Ward had defeated Owens in a 60-yard Indoor event on March 2 of that year, and again in the hurdles. In July, at the AAU Championships, Eulace

Peacock also beat Owens twice—in the 100-meter dash in 10.2 seconds and in the long jump at 26' 3". Owens and Peacock were envisioned as another one-two sprint punch for the upcoming Olympics like Tolan-Metcalfe in 1932. With this kind of talent, it is not surprising that Adolf Hitler was worried about America's "Black Auxiliaries," as he called our black runners.

As controversial as the 1936 Olympics themselves were, problems started for the American team and for Owens even before they left for Berlin. Owens suffered a few personal problems in July 1935 in California, and performed poorly at the AAU Championships in Lincoln, Nebraska. Then he got married and was later told that he may have endangered his amateur standing by accepting a job as a "page" in the Ohio House of Representatives. That taken care of, he fared badly in his studies and found himself academically ineligible for the 1935–36 indoor track season.

Compounding all these problems was a mounting campaign to boycott the 1936 Olympics. On September 15, 1935, Adolf Hitler issued the Nuremberg Laws which stripped German Jews of their citizenship rights and equal treatment under German law. The AAU then voted in the fall of 1935 to boycott unless Germany changed its treatment of their Jewish athletes. The American Olympic Committee sent several leaders—including Avery Brundage, its president—to Germany to see for themselves. They came back with high marks for the Germans. What, pray tell, raged the black press, did Brundage and his cohorts see? Brundage remained a despised figure to the majority of black athletes the rest of his days.

Black stars like Owens were also reminded by the black press that, here at home, neither the major leagues nor the National Football League admitted blacks. The New York *Amsterdam News* urged our black athletes to stay put, as did Owens' two hometown black papers, the *Cleveland Call and Post* and the *Cleveland Gazette.* To make matters worse for him, because of his troubles as a "page," the AAU ordered Owens' name removed from consideration for the Sullivan Award, given annually to the nation's most outstanding amateur athlete. Thus Owens' May 25 performance—the most acclaimed athletic feat of the century—went unrewarded by the sport's highest authorities.

Owens had to be slightly unsure since Peacock had beaten him five straight times since July 1935. But then Peacock tore a hamstring muscle at the Penn Relays on April 24, 1936, while Owens regained his form. Owens, by now at five feet ten inches and 165 pounds, broke the world mark in the 100-yard dash in 9.3 seconds on May 16, won all of his events at the Big Ten Championships, and easily qualified for the American Olympic squad at New York City's Randall's Island. His other black teammates were Ralph Metcalfe and Mack Robinson (Jackie Robinson's brother) in the sprints, David Albritton and Cornelius Johnson in the high jump, Archie Williams and James Luvalle in the 400 meters, "Long" John Woodruff in the 800 meters, Fritz Pollard, Jr. in the 110-meter hurdles, and John Brooks in the long jump. The sprinter Louise Stokes and hurdler Tydie Pickett made the women's team. Willis Ward of Michigan, Mel Walker (Owens' Ohio State teammate), and Peacock missed their berths. One favorable note was the designation of Tuskegee as the site for semi-final trials for women—a first for a black school.

The team sailed on the S.S. *Manhattan* on July 15, and arrived in Bremerhaven, Germany, nine days later. Owens was mobbed by German autograph seekers as he and his teammates tried to adjust to the time change. When the Games began a week later, everything seemed in order except for the banning of Howell King, a black boxer, for supposedly pilfering a camera from a store. Then on the very first day, what began as a perceived slight in time mushroomed into legend.

After Hitler watched two German athletes win gold medals, he ordered them to his box for personal congratulations. He did the same for a Finnish athlete. Then Cornelius Johnson won the high jump over David Albritton but Hitler left just before the playing of the American national anthem. No one will ever know for sure if Hitler was purposely avoiding a face-to-face confrontation in full public view with a black athlete, but the American press played the "snub" for all it was worth. According to William J. Baker, "Not until the next day did Owens win his first gold medal. By then the president of the International Olympic Committee, Henri de Baillet-Latour of Belgium, had gotten word to Hitler that as the head of the host government he must be impartial in his accolades.... Hitler stopped inviting winners to his stadium box."[15]

The snub to Johnson was eventually transposed to a snub to Owens that Owens himself initially denied but later erroneously admitted was true. Owens won his first gold medal on the second day,

August 3. In the semi-final heats on the first day, he broke the world record in the 100 meters at 10.2 seconds, but it was wind-aided. In the final on that Monday, he lined up against Metcalfe and Frank Wykoff of the United States, and the runners from Germany, Sweden, and the Netherlands. He drew the inside lane but officials had moved everyone one lane out because the distance runners had chewed up the lane nearest the curb. But it did not matter as Owens won by three yards in 10.3 seconds with Metcalfe second. One down, three to go.

On Tuesday morning, August 4, Owens qualified for the 200-meter finals with Mack Robinson. In both of his heats he clocked 21.1 seconds for new world marks around a turn, but trouble loomed in the afternoon long jump trials. American jumpers had won every long jump event since 1896. After Owens took a practice run through the long jump pit, an official raised his red flag to signify an attempt. Practice runs were not allowed in Germany. On his second try, his take-off foot stepped over the front edge of the board and he fouled again. He had one last try to qualify and here more legend surfaced.

Many accounts had Owens' chief rival, the German Lutz Long, as coming over to him to offer words of encouragement. In the book, *Jesse: The Man Who Outran Hitler,* Long supposedly said, "I Luz Long. I think I know what is wrong with you."[16] In actuality, Long did no such thing and Owens later admitted as much to close friends. But the first version was more dramatic and many sportswriters let him get away with this little slip. In any event, Owens qualified and set up a real confrontation with Long. Owens held a small

lead at 25' 9¾" after the first round of jumps but Long matched it. Then Owens sailed beyond 26' and Long failed to keep up. But Owens still had more in reserve though his second gold medal was already in his pocket. On his last solo try, he sprung himself out to a new Olympic record of 26' 5¼". Two down, two to go.

Both Owens and Mack Robinson qualified in the morning rain on August 5 for the 200-meter finals. In the finals in the afternoon, Owens and Robinson crouched next to two Dutchmen, a Swede, and a Canadian. With the starter's pistol Owens catapulted his lithe figure to victory in an Olympic record time of 20.7 seconds. Robinson was second in a borrowed pair of shoes in 21.1 seconds. But the attention once again centered on Owens who had just won his third gold medal, the first since 1900. Three down, one to go. He rested and watched Fritz Pollard, Jr. win a bronze medal in the 110-meter hurdles on August 6.

Ordinarily, Owens would have been finished competing, but he surprisingly found himself having to lead off the 400-meter relay team. The team was told at the Randall's Island trials that the fourth, fifth, sixth, and seventh finishers in the 100-meter trials would make up the 400-meter relay squad. That was Foy Draper, Marty Glickman, Sam Stoller, and Mack Robinson. But at the last minute the coaches changed their minds in a ploy that looked as though the two Jewish runners, Glickman and Stoller, were intentionally overlooked and that favoritism for the University of Southern California (USC) was involved.

Though Robinson had qualified for the 200 meters, he was replaced by Frank Wykoff who was a USC student. The coach of the relay squad was Dean Cromwell, also of

USC. Glickman and Stoller had resisted protests back home for going to Nazi Germany in the first place and this was another blow. In addition, Cromwell had Glickman, Stoller, and Draper run in a special 100-meter race next to the Olympic Village to see who would run in what order in the relay. Both Glickman and Stoller finished ahead of Draper in this dry run. But Lawson Robertson, the head coach, decided to drop both Glickman and Stoller in favor of Draper and Wykoff.

According to William J. Baker, Metcalfe and Wykoff thought Owens had selfishly wanted to win a fourth gold medal and had not protested the exclusion of the Jewish runners. Glickman said he vividly remembers Owens saying in a meeting: "Coach, let Marty and Sam run. I've had enough. I've won three gold medals. Let them run, they deserve it. They ought to run." To which one of the coaches snidely replied, "You'll do as you're told."[17] Back home the press concerning the benching of Glickman and Stoller was lost in the euphoria of the team's victories.

Metcalfe, who lost twice to Eddie Tolan at Los Angeles in 1932, finally got his gold medal in the relay; Archie Williams won the 400 meter dash in 46.5 seconds; John Woodruff captured the 800-meter run in 1:52.9 minutes; and James Luvalle, the only Phi Beta Kappa in the field, won a bronze medal in the 400 meters. John Brooks placed sixth in the long jump. All returned home as conquering heroes in an election year that saw black Americans courted as never before.

After a series of economic and occupational mishaps, Owens finally settled down as a representative for the Atlantic Richfield Company, while Woodruff, Pol-lard, Williams, Albritton, and Metcalfe finished college and went on to respectable lives. Luvalle earned his doctorate in chemistry and became a college professor at Stanford University. Neither Stokes nor Pickett won medals at Berlin in the women's events.

In 1950, the Associated Press named Owens as the "Athlete of the Half-Century," an especially welcomed honor since he failed to win the Sullivan Award in 1936, given to the nation's most outstanding amateur athlete. In late 1936, Owens publicly backed the losing presidential candidate, Alf Landon. He also lost his amateur standing because of oral agreements made to cash in on his Olympic fame. Not only did these offers fail to materialize, but he became involved in a series of business disasters that sullied his name for a time. His stature was resurrected by presidential appointments for world tours to promote sports and international understanding. Through it all, his wife Ruth stood by his side.

In 1972 his alma mater awarded Owens an honorary doctorate, and in 1974 the NCAA presented the Theodore Roosevelt Award to him in honor of his college contributions. He was made a charter member of the Track and Field Hall of Fame. In 1976, President Gerald Ford awarded him the highest accolade a civilian could receive—the Presidential Medal of Freedom.

The victories of black Americans at Berlin served as a beacon for all Americans of African descent. The Depression was beginning to ebb and another migration from South to North had started. More runners were competing in more events as the Second World War decimated the college campuses. But the black dominance in sprinting and jumping had begun in earnest despite the plaudits of Woodruff and Williams at Berlin. The increasingly learned coaches of young black speedsters funneled them into the shorter races so they could perform like Jesse Owens. They found inspiration in his exploits.

A host of long jumpers emulated Owens including Mel Walker of Ohio State; Edward Burke of Marquette; Albert Threadgill of Temple; Gilbert Crutcher of Colorado; Paul Robeson, Jr. of Cornell; Don Barksdale of UCLA; Joshua Williamson of Camp Plauche, Louisiana; Lloyd Thompson of Xavier; Adam Berry of Southern University; Kermit King of Pittsburgh (Kansas); William Lacefield of UCLA; and on through Herb Douglas, the AAU champion in 1945.

Said Douglas, "When I was thirteen, Jesse Owens influenced me...I had the opportunity to meet him....During the 30s...the Big Ten did not allow any Blacks to play basketball....I knew if I could go and excel in track and field, I could get an education."[18] Only in track and field at a white college before 1950 could a black athlete reach his full potential. Basketball in some conferences was closed to him, professional football banned him from 1934 until 1946, and major league baseball had him barred since 1889. He could not do any better than the cinder paths.

Nowadays, experts think back to Owens and Metcalfe and wonder which of the two was better on closer inspection. Owens won the AAU 100-meter title only once; Metcalfe won it three times. Owens failed to win the AAU 200-meter title; Metcalfe won it five times in a row. Owens won the Intercollegiate 100-yard dash twice; Metcalfe three times. And again in the Intercollegiate 220-yard dash, Owens won it twice to three times for Metcalfe. What does all this prove? Maybe nothing but the results are surprising when compared with the relative publicity they received.

Our black distance runners were not difficult to identify at all. After Archie Williams and John Woodruff came James Herbert of New York University (NYU) with a world record at 600 yards in 1:11 minutes. Woodruff was the AAU, Intercollegiate, and ICAAAA champion in the half-mile. Others who chased his trail were George Carr at Marquette, Dave Bolen at Colorado, Robert Kelly at Illinois, Reginald Pearman and Stan and Maurice Callender at NYU, among others. But on the eve of the 1948 Olympics, no black runner held a world record beyond 880 yards. Conversely, no white person had high jumped beyond 6' 9" as of 1939. Three blacks—Cornelius Johnson, David Albritton, Mel Walker—had all crossed this bar.

In the mile, only James T. Smith of Indiana University and Frank Dixon of NYU stirred passions. Smith had clocked 4:11 minutes, and Dixon had begun as a cross country star at New York City's James Monroe High School in 1938. By 1942, Dixon had captured the AAU and ICAAAA cross country titles and the AAU mile crown. As a freshman at NYU, he had a 4:9.6 minutes time under his belt in the mile. In the weight events, Bill Watson of Michigan was a Big Ten champion in the discus, long jump, and the high jump. He won the AAU decathlon in 1940 and in 1943.

It had been a glorious run for these stars on campuses where all but a select few of the black students were athletes, or sons and daughters of professionals. For most of them, athletic talents were their entry to a prestigious education and a chance for honors on the track. After World War II, there would be new hurdles—racial and athletic—to overcome. White southern schools waited until forced by legal procedures to admit blacks in the early 1970s. At other institutions where blacks had already established a presence, new and subtler barriers to free expression surfaced to make campus life horrid in the 1960s. Some of those at white schools wound up organizing the most memorable protests ever mounted by black athletes, while continuing to burn up the track. For this new generation of runners, life would be, as it was for James Cleveland Owens, "A Hard Road to Glory."

Our Club Stars

Lest we forget, there were a few runners who did not go to any college at all, or who earned their honors while representing their home clubs. These organizations filled the gaps left by the limits of black colleges and the tokenism of white schools. Many of the clubs had been formed in the first decade of this century by middle-class blacks to field track squads and basketball fives. A surprising number of them were filled with upwardly mobile West Indians who were first-generation immigrants. All of them stressed education and "social" members—those joining for status, and so on—also made up a sizable portion of the total. The overwhelming majority of these groups whose members appear in national track listings were based in New York City, Philadelphia, Boston, Washington, D.C., Chicago, western Pennsylvania, and northern New Jersey.

R. Earl Johnson, for instance, who won the AAU 10,000-meter run from 1921 to 1923, represented Thompson Steel. He made the 1920 Olympic team, but was forced to quit in the fifteenth lap due to stomach cramps. Johnson may have been the first black Olympian to write a guest column for a black newspaper—the *Afro-American*—while at the Olympics. Tom Anderson represented New York City's St. Christopher Club in the weight events in the early 1920s. Louis Watson, a high jumper from the Alpha Physical Cultural Club, just missed qualifying for the Olympic team. Black America's first pair of top-flight marathoners were also club-affiliated. Many thought Clifton Mitchell of St. Christopher should have been selected to the 1920 team. Aaron Morris of the New York Runners club finished in sixth place in the Boston Marathon on April 19, 1919.

Cecil Cook, who won the 1925 AAU 400-meter run, represented Salem-Crescent, one of the oldest black clubs from Brooklyn. Louise Stokes, who was on the 1932 Olympic team, was a member of the Onteona Athletic Club in Malden, Massachusetts. The prowess of the Mercury Athletic Club members has been previously mentioned. As early as the 1920s, some athletes ran for their schools from September through the following June and then for a club. Ned Gourdin of Harvard ran for the racially integrated Dorchester Athletic Club of Boston in the summers.

A thorny problem for black clubs was their inability to receive AAU accreditation. Authorities simply refused to grant the credibility which ensued to sanctioned clubs. William DeHart Hubbard finally secured the first such sanction in 1926. This official recognition meant that clubs could then enter teams in AAU meets; they could hold meets themselves provided certain minimum standards were met; and they could certainly use their status to attract the best runners as members. When club memberships were impractical, some ran unattached. Archie Harris, for example, won the AAU discus title in 1941 though he belonged to no club. But that was rare and usually occurred in weight events.

The inability of blacks to form AAU-affiliated clubs in the South seriously hampered their track progress until well into the 1950s. Most efforts centered around the black colleges, but unless there were dynamic organizers like Cleveland Abbott to run them, a void resulted. In fact, not a single black AAU-affiliated club representative won a national title prior to World War II. However, the list of black national winners from northern clubs is lengthy, as is the list of southern-based black baseball teams. The irony is that while major league berths were barred to blacks until 1946, they nevertheless formed dozens of teams in the South. Track imposed no limits but southern blacks failed to show enough interest to take advantage of the opportunities. Against this background, the success of the Tuskegee women's squad in the late 1930s and early 1940s is even more extraordinary, coming as it did with exclusively home-grown talent.

After the war, club membership assumed more importance since the available college scholarships were limited at a time of increasing demand. But the commercialization of the sport at every level and the developing rivalry with the Soviets provided a niche for clubs with quality programs, quality coaches, and state-of-the-art facilities. Colleges just could not turn out enough record-breaking perfor-

mers. Later, as track participation became a vocation like any other with stipends and appearance fees, clubs dominated the list of national winners. For the black athlete, it all began in the early 1900s with far-sighted groups like Smart Set, St. Christopher, Alpha Physical Culture, Wissahickon Boys Club, and Salem-Crescent. A tremendous debt is owed them for leading the way.

The sustained success of black track and field performers between the two World Wars is well documented. Unlike baseball, football, and basketball, track—along with boxing to a large degree—allowed blacks to demonstrate their talents and be judged accordingly. Perhaps because the judging of track races is so objective, it was relatively difficult for white authorities to deny any talented runner his or her rightful place on the starting line. International competition such as the Olympics also served to force American officials to field the best team, regardless of ethnic or religious backgrounds. But, as just mentioned, two Jewish athletes at the 1936 Olympics—Sam Stoller and Marty Glickman—were denied opportunities in the 400-meter relay because a coach favored his own college pupil. This had happened to blacks for generations.

The post-World War II era is characterized by an all-out assault on the record books. More scientific methods of training, the sub-discipline of exercise physiology—unheard of in 1945—and computer analysis would result in new training procedures and techniques. Super performances from super athletes ensued as the Olympic Games were joined by other competitions like the Pan-American Games, the Asian Games, the Pan-African Games, the World

University Games, and the Commonwealth Games, among others, to show the world just how far, how fast, and how high men and women can truly move.

Notes

1. *New York Age*, 14 May 1927.
2. *California Eagle*, 14 March 1930.
3. Nolan Thaxton, *Documentary Analysis of Women's Track at Tuskegee and Tennessee State* (Tuskegee University, formerly Tuskegee Institute, Tuskegee, Alabama), p. 66.
4. *California Eagle*, 13 June 1925.
5. *Boston Telegram*, 25 May 1921.
6. *New York Telegram*, 21 August 1921.
7. *Chicago Defender*, 6 September 1930.
8. Henderson, *The Negro in Sports*, p. 54.
9. John Behee, *Hail to the Victors!* (Ann Arbor, Michigan: Ulrich's Books, 1974), p. 17.
10. William J. Baker, *Jesse Owens: An American Life* (New York: The Free Press, 1986), p. 12.
11. Ibid., p. 35.
12. Ibid.
13. *Norfolk Journal and Guide*, 8 June 1935.
14. *New York Times*, 2 June 1935.
15. Baker, *Jesse Owens: An American Life*, pp. 90-91.
16. Jesse Owens, *The Man Who Outran Hitler* (New York: Fawcett Gold Medal Books, 1978), p. 71.
17. Baker, *Jesse Owens: An American Life*, p. 104.
18. *Dollars and Sense* magazine (June-July 1983), p. 28.

CHAPTER 3

SINCE 1945

In the immediate post-World War II era, black track stars were known for their sprinting and jumping. Jesse Owens and his black Olympic teammates had helped America to a team victory in Berlin in 1936. However, by 1948, no black runners held world records for distances greater than 880 yards. (Some critics charged that blacks were genetically built for shorter races.) But in the hurdles, it was imagined that they *should* excel, since this event involved jumping over ten rather short obstacles as fast as possible. Not so. Though, on paper, blacks seemed suited for it, only a handful had mastered the techniques to set world-class marks, and it was also viewed as an event for those who could not make the "first team" in the 100-yard and 220-yard dashes. But for William Harrison Dillard of Baldwin-Wallace College, such talk made no difference.

Coming on strong in the late 1940s, Dillard tied the American record in 1946 in the 220-yard hurdles at 22.5 seconds. That same year, he won the AAU 200-meter hurdles title at 23.3 seconds, a new AAU record. He repeated the feat with an identical time in 1947. Elmore Harris, formerly of Morgan State and later with the Shore Athletic Club of New Jersey, had been AAU 200-meter hurdles winner in 1944, the same year he was AAU 400-

meter champion. Indoors, he claimed three AAU titles before the 1948 London Olympics.

In the weight events, blacks had never made much headway. No black man has won an Olympic medal in the discus, shot put, or javelin as of the 1992 Barcelona Games. Theodore Cable had a chance in 1912, but was injured; and Thomas Anderson in 1920 failed to place. In the shot put, Lilburn Williams of Xavier University had tossed the 16-pound shot 53 feet 7 inches in 1939 to win the AAU Outdoor title, a first for a black-college athlete. This distance would have won the event in the 1936 Berlin Olympics. But help was on the way.

Woodrow "Woody" Strode of UCLA recorded heaves of 51-feet 6-inches; Archie Harris had noteworthy tosses while attending Indiana University; and Bill Watson of the University of Michigan placed in the shot put in the NCAA's. The best ever, however, was Charles Fonville of the University of Michigan, who was a coholder of the world record set on April 17, 1948, at 58-feet ¼-inch. Fonville set his record at the Kansas Relays in Lawrence, after being forced to stay in private housing in the black section of the city. Earlier, he and Harrison Dillard had been assured that they could stay with their teammates. Incensed, Dillard also proceeded to set a world record of 13.6 seconds in the 110-meter high hurdles in the same arena. New records; same old racism. Fonville, who like Jesse Owens paid his own way through college, injured his back just two weeks after his record toss and could not try out for the 1948 Olympic squad. Those black athletes who *did* make the Olympic team represented the widest range of talent ever seen.

1948: The XIVth Olympiad at London, England

A record 4,062 athletes from fifty-eight nations participated in the 1948 Olympics in London, England, amidst a continuing buildup from the rubble of World War II bombings. One hundred and thirty-eight events were held between July 29 and August 14. Fifty-eight black American athletes sailed for London with their teammates aboard the *S. S. America*.

Pre-Olympic hopes in the black community were very high. Most people expected many medals from the fifty-eight-member black contingent, but these self-same supporters failed to take into account the general improvement of training methods and athletes around the world. In the end, blacks returned with eight gold, two silver, and three bronze medals in track and field.

The twenty-five-year-old Dillard, nicknamed "Bones" by his friends, provided the major surprise among the men. He had come into the 1948 AAU Nationals with eighty-two consecutive hurdles victories, but failed to qualify for the U.S. team. He got to London by finishing third in the 100-meters and then won the gold medal.

Noted Dillard: "I was twenty-five years old when I made the team. It was the realization of a childhood dream and it is about as far as the amateur athlete can go . . . I remember standing on the victory stand facing the huge scoreboards at the end of the stadium. I remember standing at attention seeing the flag being raised before some 75,000–80,000 people, including the King and Queen of England. I could feel the hair stand up on the back of my neck. It was a tremendous feeling. It was almost as if I could feel my whole athletic life flickering in front of me."[1]

Malvin Whitfield of Ohio State was simply the best combination 400–800 meter runner of his day. In June of 1948, he began a six-year period in which he would lose only three of sixty-nine races at either 800 meters or 880 yards. Like Dillard, he went on to win more medals in the 1952 Olympics.

Harold Norwood "Barney" Ewell, of Penn State, was thirty years old when he won his medals. (In the 4 x 100-meter relay, Ewell was part of a squad that was three-quarters black. The white member was Mel Patton.) He was also an accomplished broad jumper. Unfortunately, he lost his amateur status just after the Olympic Games for accepting an excessive number of prizes from grateful townsfolk in his native Harrisburg, Pennsylvania.

William S. "Willie" Steele followed the path left by a former West Coast jumper Cornelius Johnson. Six years before, Steele was the AAU Junior broad jump winner. He was the 1947 AAU and NCAA titleholder, and in 1948 after winning the NCAA title again, he became only the second jumper in history—apart from Jesse Owens—to break the 26-foot barrier twice. He attended San Jose State.

Lorenzo Christopher Wright competed for Wayne State College and, like Dillard, backed into the team. He was primarily a broad jumper, but finished fourth at the Olympics. On the relay team, he was a last-minute substitute for Ed Conwell, who had an asthma attack.

Herbert Paul Douglas, Jr., hailed from the University of Pittsburgh. At the Olympic Trials he gave his career-best leap of 25 feet 3 inches, but could not repeat the distance in London. He came within one inch of finishing second.

Edward Conwell and Dave Bolen were also members of the track and field squad, but did not place.

A monumental milestone was reached when Alice Coachman (Davis) became the first black woman to win a gold medal in Olympic competition. She had the added distinction of being the only American woman to win a gold medal in track and field at that Olympiad. She still holds the record for most victories without a loss in the national AAU Outdoor High Jump—ten in a row between 1939 and 1948. She attended both Tuskegee and Albany State. Coachman is a member of the National Track and Field Hall of Fame, the Helms Hall of Fame, the Black Athletes Hall of Fame, the Tuskegee Hall of Fame, the Georgia State Hall of Fame, and the Bob Douglas Hall of Fame.

Audrey Mickey Patterson of Tennessee State College began that school's streak of female Olympic medalists. At the Trials, she finished second in the 100-meters and won the 200-meters. She failed to make the finals in the 100-meters in London.

There were seven blacks on the women's squad, all from either Tuskegee or Tennessee State. Besides Coachman, others from Tuskegee included Theresa Manuel, Nell Jackson (who in 1956 became the first black head track coach of an American Olympic team), and Mabel Walker. Heriwentha Mae Faggs and Emma Reed were Patterson's teammates from Tennessee State. Faggs, who was only sixteen years old, was eliminated in the semifinals of the 200-meters.

The 1948 Olympics marked the end of an extraordinary period in black track exploits. In the sixteen years between the Olympic Games in 1932 and 1948, blacks established their supremacy in the sprints and jumping events, and served notice that the distance and weight events were not out of reach. While the next twenty years witnessed more victories, higher black expectations would be met with stiffening resistance from collegiate and Olympic authorities. More importantly, sports like track and field became valuable adjuncts to the maturing civil rights movement which swept the nation.

At the end of the war, the leadership roles of the YMCA's and church teams had been superseded by well-organized clubs, Police Athletic League competitions, and college teams. Blacks who did not or could not attend college were forced to find clubs that would accept them. The black college itself was beginning to lose its elitist image in the black community, but its track and field facilities paralleled the degree of sophistication of its football program. Football and track athletes used the same field, so if the football field was modern, the track facilities would be the same.

Still, as late as 1948, even the best-equipped black schools had serious shortcomings. There was, except in rare cases, little expertise in distance coaching; records made on black tracks were not recognized internationally; training equipment was seldom state of the art.

Two years later, black track stars were given a taste of a future problem in which they were to play a major role. In June 1950, following the AAU Championships held at the University of Maryland and at Morgan State College (the first National AAU meet held at a black school), selections were made for international teams to travel to Europe and South Africa. One black athlete listed South Africa as his fifth choice but was turned down, and AAU authorities were criticized for deliberately keeping blacks off the team because this country practiced overt racial segregation.

The AAU had last sent a team to South Africa in 1931, but the public announcement of that country's official racial policy of "apartheid" in 1948 had provided critics with new weapons of protest. The official 1950 AAU squad was all-white.

Politics aside, black and white track athletes could not have imagined what lay ahead: The sheer number of events would increase fifty percent, especially for women; new competitions like the Pan-Am Games would surface; new sanctioning bodies like the Association for Intercollegiate Athletics for Women (AIAW) and the National Association of Intercollegiate Athletics (NAIA) would be organized; the National Collegiate Athletic Association (NCAA) would subdivide according to enrollment size and degree of participation; and the growth of the junior and community college system would provide more opportunities to compete.

But the grandest competition of them all, the Olympic Games, would continue to bring together the world's best athletes every four years and provide a common denominator around which the entire planet could peacefully focus, at least, for two weeks.

1952: The XVth Olympiad at Helsinki, Finland

This second Olympiad since World War II was significant because it marked the first appearance of a team from the Soviet Union. The United States was caught up in the "red scare," brought about in part by Senator Joseph McCarthy, who held accusatory hearings and suspected Communist infiltration in every government department. Even *Ebony* magazine, the most widely read periodical in the black community, joined the bandwagon in headlining an article entitled "Can Negro Athletes Stop The Russians?"

The white American Olympian Bob Mathias noted, "There were many more pressures on the American athletes because of the Russians than in 1948. They were in a sense the real enemies. You just loved to beat 'em. You just had to beat 'em."[2]

However, Milton Campbell, the black silver medalist in the 1952 Olympic Decathlon, said, "We [black athletes] didn't make that big a deal of it."[3]

Strangely, the United States at the time had no well-coordinated program to train Olympic athletes. Training was left entirely to schools, clubs, and the AAU. The Pan-Am Games were organized in 1951 for the first time as a prelude to the Olympics themselves. (The Pan-Am Games would be held every four years in the year preceding the Olympic Games.) The American contingent was part of a total of 5,294 men and 573 women to compete at Helsinki.

Black Americans won fourteen medals at Helsinki. Their results are shown in the Reference section.

For Harrison Dillard, known as "Bones," his were the third and fourth gold medals in successive Olympiads. Called by General George Patton "the best goddamn athlete I've ever seen,"[4] Dillard was 5-feet 10-inches and weighed only 150 pounds. He had attended East Technical High School in Cleveland, Ohio, the same school that had produced Jesse Owens, and Baldwin-Wallace College. Though acknowledged as the greatest hurdler of his time, Dillard missed qualifying in his specialty event for the 1948 Olympic team; he made the team as a sprinter and won the 100-meter dash.

After that 1948 Olympic win, Dillard's black teammate Norwood "Barney" Ewell cried out, "I won, I did it!" But the Panamanian Lloyd LaBeach told him "No, Bones win."[5] Dillard's victories in 1952, however, were never in doubt. He finished his career with fourteen AAU and six NCAA National titles.

The 1952 Olympiad was also the second for Mal Whitfield, an Ohio State University product. Undoubtedly the finest 400/800-meter runner of his time, between June 1948 and October 1954 Whitfield lost only three of sixty-nine races of 800 meters or 880 yards.

He repeated as gold medalist in the 1952 Olympic Games 800-meter run. He eventually captured five AAU titles and five indoor and outdoor world records. In the late fifties and early sixties, he spent time in Africa training various Olympic teams. In 1955, he was the first black recipient of the James E. Sullivan Award, given to the nation's premier amateur athlete.

Andrew Stanfield, a graduate of Seton Hall University, represented the New York Pioneer Athletic Club. In addition to capturing six IC4A titles in the 100-yard and 60-yard dashes, he set a world record of 20.6 seconds in the 220-yard dash in 1951.

Jerome Biffle won the NCAA long jump title in 1950 while at the University of Denver. When he won his Olympic gold medal, he was an Army private.

Mae Faggs started out in a New York PAL program and later attended Tennessee State, where she was coached by Ed Temple. She won five AAU titles in the 100/200-meters and a gold and a silver medal in the 1955 Pan-Am Games. She was given credit by Wilma Rudolph for providing invaluable assistance during Rudolph's career.

Catherine Hardy attended Fort Valley State in Georgia. She won three AAU indoor and outdoor titles.

Barbara Jones was, at fifteen years and one hundred twenty-three days, the youngest American female to win an Olympic gold medal in track and field. She started in the Chicago Catholic Youth Organization (CYO) and attended Tennessee State. Jones won three AAU titles between 1953 and 1957.

Meredith Gourdine went to Cornell, where he won the IC4A long jump title and the 220-yard hurdles in 1951. He finished ahead of Biffle in the trials and at the AAU, but had to settle for second in Helsinki. The initial favorite in the long jump was George Brown of UCLA. But Brown, who is black, fouled three straight times during the finals at Helsinki.

Milton Campbell was a seventeen-year-old high school student from Plainfield, New Jersey, when he won his 1952 Olympic silver medal. He also won the 1953 AAU Decathlon title, with 7,235 points. Harold Bruguiere, his high school coach, said, "He is beyond a doubt the greatest athlete in all around ability I have ever seen."[6] Inexplicably, he noted, "No black college ever contacted me—none. I had sixty-three offers but no offers from a black school."[7] This has to be one of the most serious oversights by black colleges in track history.

Ollie Matson who attended the University of San Francisco, tried to make the 1948 United States Olympic team in the 400-meters, but failed. he did win two medals at the 1952 Games. Better known for his football prowess, he played professionally for the Chicago Cardinals, the Los Angeles Rams, the Detroit Lions, and the Philadelphia Eagles.

1956: The XVIth Olympiad at Melbourne, Australia

The success of black athletes at Helsinki was shown on television and on movie newsreels. Only Joe Louis and Sugar Ray Robinson enjoyed much international adulation at the time. For Mae Faggs, Catherine Hardy, and Barbara Jones, their gold medals represented the height of acclaim for black female athletes. The 1952 United States Women's Olympic squad consisted of only ten athletes (and a manager) competing in only nine events. Nineteen fifty-six would be different.

Among black colleges, Morgan State continued in its premier role, especially in relay events. In 1955, the state team won the AAU Indoor relay crown. On May 6, 1954, Roger Bannister of England finally broke the four-minute barrier in the mile—3:59.4, only to see it broken six weeks later on June 21 by John Landy in 3:58.

Ted Corbitt, the black marathoner, enjoyed

success in winning the 1954 AAU Philadelphia and Detroit marathons. Another notable showing was a sixth-place finish in the 1952 Boston marathon. In 1955, at age thirty-five, he finished tenth in a field of 160 at Boston.

Noteworthy for blacks were three political events that took place between the 1952 and 1956 Games. First, President Harry S. Truman desegregated the Armed Forces, thereby desegregating its sports programs and guaranteeing the best training and coaching possible for black GIs. Second, in a monumental 1954 United States Supreme Court decision, the justices declared that "separate but equal" public schooling for blacks and whites was unconstitutional. It was immediately assumed by many that black students would soon enjoy the same athletic opportunities as white students.

The third event affected the 1956 Games more directly. Before the Games began in November, the Soviet Union invaded Hungary, and Great Britain, France, and Israel seized the Suez Canal from Egypt. Holland, Spain, and Switzerland withdrew from the Games over the Soviet invasion, and Lebanon, Iraq, and Egypt withdrew over the Suez seizure. The International Olympic Committee tried to remain aloof from it all.

America's black athletes took notice of these incidents, trained hard, and returned with eighteen medals. These medalists are listed in the Reference section.

Milton Campbell, who attended Indiana University, won the gold medal in the decathlon. Surprisingly, he attempted only five decathlons during his career—the Olympic Trials in 1952 and 1956, the Olympics in 1952 and 1956, and the 1953 AAU which he won. He considered himself a hurdler first and a decathlete second.

Lee Calhoun became the first black male athlete from a black college to win an Olympic gold medal. Trained by the famed black coach at North Carolina Central, Dr. Leory

Walker, Calhoun set an Olympic record and is the only man to win two Olympic high hurdles titles. He also won AAU, NAIA, and NCAA titles in 1956 and 1957. After a brief suspension of his amateur status, he won his third AAU and a Pan-Am title in 1959.

At the 1956 Olympic Trials, Charles Dumas was the first human to break the seven-foot barrier in the high jump. He had tied for first place in the high jump at the 1955 AAUs, but won it outright in 1957–59. Representing the University of Southern California, he finished sixth in the 1960 Games.

Greg Bell won the 1955 AAU Long Jump title and added the NCAA title in the 1956–57 and the AAU Indoor title in 1958.

Charles Jenkins was a surprise Olympic winner in the 400-meter run. His teammate, Lou Jones, had set a world record during the Trials at 45.2 seconds, but could do no better than fifth place in Melbourne. Jones led for most of the race, but was passed by four runners near the end. A Villanova University student, Jenkins won the AAU title in 1955, the IC4A title in 1955 and 1957 and set a world record for the 500-yard run in 1956. He eventually succeeded his college coach, Jumbo Elliot, at Villanova.

Lou Jones partly atoned for his lapse in the 400-meter run by sharing victory in the 1600-meter relay along with Jenkins and white teammates Jesse Mashburn and Thomas Courtney. A graduate of Manhattan College, he set his first world record in the 400-meter run at the 1955 Pan-Am Games.

Ira Murchison and Leamon King shared gold medals in the 400-meter relay with Thane Baker and Bobby Morrow. Murchison, who stood only 5-feet 5-inches, ran for both Iowa and Western Michigan and in 1956 set a world record of 10.1 seconds in the 100-meters at a military meet in Berlin, Germany. This graduate of Wendell Phillips High in Chicago also won the AAU 60-yard title in 1957 and the NCAA 100-yard title in 1958.

King set a world record of 9.3 seconds for the 100-yard dash in 1956 and won the AAU title in 1957.

Rafer Johnson won the AAU decathlon in 1956 and, after winning a silver medal in Melbourne, he never lost again. He also qualified for the 1956 Games in the long jump, but did not participate because of injury.

Andrew Stanfield returned to capture a silver medal in his second Olympics and Josh Culbreath of Morgan State captured a bronze in the 400-meter hurdles. Culbreath was AAU champion in 1953–55. In 1957 at Oslo, Norway, he set a world record of 50.5 seconds in the 440-yard hurdles. He was black America's first premier intermediate hurdler.

The women's squad, coached by Nell Jackson of Tuskegee Institute (now Tuskegee University), produced its first Olympic and world record by a black American female in the person of Mildred McDaniel. Not only did Mildred set a world and Olympic record, she also defeated the former record holder, Iolanda Balas of Roumania. Three years later, McDaniel won the high jump at the Pan-Am Games.

Willye White, nicknamed "Red," participated in a record five Olympiads and won medals in two—1956 and 1964 (a silver medal in the 400-meter relay). She won the AAU Outdoor long jump title ten times and in 1962, the Indoor title. A graduate of Tennessee State University, White also won the Pan-Am long jump title in 1963. She was truly one of America's greatest female athletes.

Mae Faggs, Isabelle Daniels, and Wilma Rudolph all hailed from Tennessee State and were coached by Ed Temple. Along with Margret Matthews, who held the American record of 19-feet 9¼-inches in the long jump, the three Tigerbelles from Tennessee State finished third in the 400-meter relay behind Australia and Great Britain. Daniels won twelve AAU Indoor and Outdoor sprint titles.

But better days lay ahead for Wilma Rudolph. One of twenty-two children from Clarksville, Tennessee, she had a deformed left foot as a child and wore a brace on her right leg for five years between the ages of seven and twelve. She was only sixteen when she participated at Melbourne. She shared in the bronze medal in the 400-meter relay after being eliminated in a preliminary heat in the 200-meter run.

1960: The XVIIth Olympiad at Rome, Italy

America wrestled with internal racial contradictions during the four years between the XVIth and the XVIIth Olympiads. What observers thought would be a peaceful transition from segregation to integration in public schools, as ordered by the Supreme Court, was not the case. In school systems where the change did take place, black coaches were usually assigned secondary positions.

Black colleges, however, made historic advances. For the first time, NAIA titles were won in basketball, baseball, football, and track in this four-year period. The familiarity of the black college coach, such as Ed Temple of Tennessee State (who succeeded Nell Jackson as Head Women's Track Coach for the 1960 United States Olympic squad), with international competition had paid off.

No group made greater strides during these forty-eight months than black female track stars. They seemed to be more team-oriented than their male counterparts and relied more on the advice of their coaches. Even travel to meets was now more bearable, because these athletes went as a group rather than as individuals. No black female—no matter how good she was—wanted to go to a strange place alone.

Nell Jackson recalls that "the distance we traveled on our way to a meet was determined by how far the next black college was from our location. Because we had no public places to stay in the fifties, we relied on the South's black colleges to house us."[8]

These considerations were of paramount importance, and it is not difficult to understand why the black colleges rather than the predominantly white colleges nurtured the first generations of black female track stars. Subsequently, Fred Thompson, who began his Atoms Track Club in 1959 as a coed venture in Brooklyn, New York, soon dropped his young male runners and concentrated solely on training the girls. Says Thompson, ". . . I had to phase out the boys because by the time they got into high school they had other things to interest them. But at that time, there wasn't one intramural program for girls' athletics."[9] Because of the increased interest in track among girls in the public schools, the USOC created a Women's Advisory Board in 1958.

With renewed vigor, black athletes came to Rome and won more gold medals than ever.

Rafer Johnson had the honor of carrying the American flag during the opening ceremonies in Rome. He must have drawn even more competitive inspiration from this experience because he set a new Olympic record in the decathlon. After his retirement from track, he became very involved in community programs in California. He was with Democratic presidential candidate Robert F. Kennedy the night he was assassinated in Los Angeles in 1968. It was Johnson who grabbed the pistol from the hands of Kennedy's assassin, Sirhan Sirhan. At the 1984 Los Angeles Games, Johnson was accorded the honor of lighting the Olympic torch above the Coliseum.

Ralph Boston won medals in three Olympiads—a gold in 1960, a silver in 1964, and a bronze in 1968. Just before the Rome Olympics in August, Boston broke Jesse Owens' long jump record with a leap of 26 feet 11¼ inches. In 1961, he broke his own world

record two more times and, in 1964 and 1965, he broke the record three additional times.

As of 1992, Boston and Edwin Moses had been the only track athletes to break a world record on six occasions.

Boston also won the AAU Outdoor long-jump title six straight years (1961 to 66) and the Indoor title in 1961. As a Tennessee State student, he won the NCAA Outdoor title in 1960. Throughout his career, he was one of the most highly respected athletes in the sport, and was known for encouraging other athletes during difficult times.

Otis Davis, from Tuscaloosa, Alabama, was a Sergeant in the Air Force in 1960. Though he never ran in an organized race until he was twenty-five, he later became the fourth black Olympian to set a world record. Davis attended the University of Oregon as a basketball player and then discovered his sprinting talents.

Willie May came into his own in his senior year at Indiana University. He finished second to Lee Calhoun in the 1960 Olympic Trials and the Games.

Lester Carney enjoyed football more than track. Playing for Ohio University, he was later drafted by the Baltimore Colts but never played professional ball.

Irvin Roberson, who attended Cornell, won the 1959 Pan-Am Games long-jump title and came very close to winning the title at Rome. He later played professional football for six years at San Diego, Oakland, Buffalo, and Miami.

Hayes Jones won six AAU hurdles titles and, from March 1959 through 1964, fifty-five consecutive indoor races. He was also Pan-Am and NCAA champion in 1959. This hurdler had such speed that he was part of the 1961 world-record 400-meter relay team. In 1964 he finally won a gold medal in the 110-meter hurdles.

John Thomas, along with Ray Norton, was a hard luck story at Rome. He was the first man to exceed 7 feet indoors, when he leaped 7 feet 1¼ inches in 1959. He was only seventeen. Coming into Rome, the 6-foot 4¾-inch Thomas had jumped over 7 feet thirty-seven times, but had to settle for a bronze medal. He explained, "When I passed [his turn] at 6 feet 11½ inches, it wasn't a psychological maneuver. I always liked to go up in two-inch increments . . . I'd never heard of any of the Russian jumpers . . . Brumel . . . we were 5-5 over the years . . . it was always the U.S. versus Russia. Freedom versus Communism. Us versus them. It was the only barometer."[10]

Thomas' reference to Valeri Brumel was an explanation of his 1964 Tokyo Olympic loss. Though both jumpers reached 7-feet 1¾-inch at Tokyo, Brumel won because of fewer misses. Thomas won seven AAU Indoor and Outdoor titles, two NCAA titles and six IC4A Indoor and Outdoor titles while at Boston University.

Other 1960 Rome disappointments were Ray Norton's last-place finishes in the 100-meter and 200-meter dashes. Norton, who attended San Jose State, had run 10.1 seconds for the 100-meter and 20.1 seconds for the 200-meter runs. To worsen matters, he caused his 400-meter relay team to be disqualified because of a bad baton pass that caused Stone Johnson to miss out on a gold medal.

Norton had an explanation for his miserable showing. At an Olympic tune-up meet before Rome, he recalls, ". . . John Thomas found out I was afraid of snakes. He came up behind me with a garter snake and held it up to my face. I jumped so high, I wrenched my lower back . . . I got to Rome with a bad case of dysentery from a train ride . . . in ten days, I went from 187 pounds to 167 . . ."[11]

No such bad luck befell Wilma Rudolph or her 400-meter relay teammates. Rudolph captivated the world with three gold medal performances, and she became the first black female to win a gold medal in a sprint event. Though she sprained her ankle the day before

her first race, she won the 100-meter final by six yards. She won the 200-meter final in the rain.

Rudolph received much encouragement along the way. At the Penn Relays one year, Jackie Robinson told the then unheralded young runner, ". . . don't let anything, or anybody, keep you from running. Keep running."[12] She won the AAU 100-meter title four straight years, from 1959 to 1962, the 200-meter title in 1960, and three AAU Indoor titles.

More than any other athlete, Rudolph is credited with stirring interest among females in track events. Noted Nell Jackson, "Wilma's accomplishments opened up the real door for women in track because of her grace and beauty. People saw her as beauty in motion."[13] To help underprivileged children she later formed the Wilma Rudolph Foundation in Indianapolis, Indiana.

Rudolph's teammates, Martha Hudson, Lucinda Williams, and Barbara Jones, all attended Tennessee State. Hudson won the AAU Indoor 100-yard title in 1959; Williams won AAU 220-yard titles in 1957–59; and Jones won AAU 100-meter titles in 1953 and 1954 and the 100-yard title in 1957.

Earlene Brown is still the only American woman to win a medal in the shot put. She won eight AAU National titles and Pan-Am Games gold medals in 1959 in the shot put and discus. Brown set American records in 1960 with a 54-foot 9¼-inch shot put and a discus throw of 176 feet 10 inches.

1964: The XVIIIth Olympiad at Tokyo, Japan

Black colleges made concerted efforts to upgrade their track programs in the early sixties. Three different schools won NAIA titles between 1960 and 1964. Public school integration of athletic teams proceeded according to local custom, but black tracksters continued to concentrate on the sprinting and jumping events. The sit-ins, protest marches, and economic boycotts so typical of this period in American history had more influence on college sports than public-school sports.

Internationally, South Africa had participated in the 1960 Olympics for the last time, but there were last-minute attempts to include them in 1964. Soviet delegates to the IOC first made protests over South Africa's presence in 1960. Black activist/comedian, Dick Gregory, called for an international boycott of the 1960 Games. He was joined in this view in 1964 by Mal Whitfield who said in an *Ebony* magazine article in 1963, ". . . It is time for American Negro athletes to join the civil rights fight—a fight that is far from won."[14] Both Gregory and Whitfield recognized a connection between the treatment of blacks in America and in South Africa.

Black American athletes left Tokyo in 1964 with nineteen American and world records to their credit. The medalists are listed in the Reference section.

Bob Hayes was awesome in winning the 100-meters by a 7-foot margin. In the 400-meter relay final, he ran the anchor leg and made up a 9-yard deficit to win ahead of the Frenchman, Jocelyn DeLecour. Hayes, who attended Florida A&M University, and ran in an awkward style, said of his Olympic performance, "It's the most satisfying feeling I've ever had in athletics." San Jose State coach Bud Winter added, ". . . he ran like he was pounding grapes into wine."[15]

Hayes, 5-foot 11-inches and 186 pounds at the time, performed the impossible on the last leg of the 400-meter relay final. Richard Stebbins, who ran the third leg in the relay, remembered that "The Japanese are reserved people. But they came to their feet, even those in the Emperor's box."[16] Some people say Hayes actually clocked 8.6 seconds for his last leg to make up the 9-yard deficit.

Hayes' standard reply to those who considered him the fastest of "The World's Fastest Humans" was, "I'm just a country boy goin' to the city with taps on my tennis shoes."[17]

Henry Carr was a superb sprinter. Besides winning the NCAA 220-yard title in 1963 for Arizona State and the AAU title in 1964, he twice set world records in the 200-meter— 20.3 seconds in 1963 and 20.2 a year later. He was the best 200/400-meter runner of his time.

As a student at Villanova, Paul Drayton was part of the 1961 400-meter relay team that set a world record of 39.1 seconds. He was the AAU 200-meter champion in 1961 and 1962.

John Rambo, who attended Long Beach State in California, was the 1964 NCAA high jump title holder and won the AAU Indoor title in 1967 and 1969.

Ulis Williams was Henry Carr's teammate at Arizona State. He was part of the 1600-meter relay teams that won the AAU title in 1962 and 1963, the NCAA title in 1963, and tied for the 1964 NCAA title.

Wyomia Tyus of Tennessee State is the only Olympian to successfully defend the 100-meter title. She is tied with Wilma Rudolph and Valerie Brisco-Hooks for most gold medals by a female runner—three. She is tied with Rudolph for most medals—four. She also won five AAU titles at 100-meters, 100-yards, 200-meters, and 200-yards; three AAU Indoor 60-yard titles; and was Pan-Am champion in 1967 at 200-meters. She could lay fair claim to the title of "Greatest American Female Olympian."

Edith McGuire was only the second black female to win three medals at the same Olympiad. She was also an accomplished long jumper, winning this event at the AAU Indoor and Outdoor meets in 1963. She was also AAU 200-meter champion in 1964 and Indoor champion in 1965 and 1966.

Marilyn White won the AAU 220-yard Indoor title in 1963 as a student at UCLA. She ran the third leg on the 400-meter relay team at Tokyo.

Changing Conditions: In the mid-sixties, black track stars faced a world different from that of their predecessors fifteen years before. The rivalry with the Soviet Union was in high gear; the USOC was much more organized, although the despised Avery Brundage was still firmly in charge; television coverage made national heroes of some athletes overnight; the national political atmosphere was charged with the black social revolution; black colleges were starting to feel the negative effects of inflation on their athletic budgets; black female track stars were, in the words of the black writer Maya Angelou, "sheroes"; the track calendar was crowded with more events, meets, and more records; and the sport itself continued to lure most of its black performers from the black underclass.

By now, black athletes had an emotional attachment to the sprinting and jumping events. Among themselves they considered it culturally treasonous to lose in these specialty contests. Whether or not they believed the theories were true.

When interviewed by *Newsweek* magazine, Tommy Smith replied, "Everything is hustle and bustle for a young black. Run to the bus, run with other kids, run from the cops. Maybe that's how we get so good at sprinting."[18] In the same issues of *Newsweek*, a white pole-vaulter countered by saying blacks did not go in for other events ". . . because distance running and vaulting are too much work for them."[19]

Said Lee Evans, the Olympic gold medalist: "We were bred for it. Certainly the black people who survived in the slave ships must have contained a high proportion of the strongest."[20] Though Evans and others like him *believed* this line of reasoning was incorrect, this did not deter negative thinking.

In 1988, Jimmy "The Greek" Snyder lost his job as a CBS sports analyst for making a similar slave breeding analogy. Snyder apologized for making the "offensive" comments.

Only a handful of black track athletes wrote their autobiographies, but from those that did, a sobering portrait can be drawn. Most of them came from broken homes, were chronic truants, cared little about school initially, were exploited at the predominantly white colleges, and had little if any attention paid to them after their usefulness was exhausted.

Bob Beamon, for instance, ". . . lived in a crowded ghetto apartment with his stepfather and his stepfather's wife, his grandmother and his great-grandfather and, eventually, two stepbrothers and a stepsister."[21]

Vince Matthews, a gold medalist in the 1968 Games, spoke for many other blacks when he said of his more fortunate black colleague, Wayne Collett, ". . . some people had said that Wayne didn't have the will to go all the way, that his black middle-class background and taste for good wines, classical and Oriental music and smart clothes didn't jive with the demands of a race like the 400 [meters]."[22] Matthews' comment was more a generalization than a stab at Collett.

Many were painted as hedonists. Bob Beamon began drinking alcohol at age seven and graduated to marijuana and wine before straightening out. John Carlos did the same. They were, as Beamon wrote, "desperate for attention."[23] Of course, not all black track athletes were like this, thanks in large measure to black college coaches and some caring white coaches as well.

It is thus easier to understand why most of the supreme public sacrifices made by black athletes were by those who felt they had little to lose. Against this backdrop, the buildup to the 1968 Olympic Games began.

The Olympic Project for Human Rights: There were more angry black athletes in more sports in the mid-sixties than at any other time. Challenges to authority and protests over discriminatory practices were everyday occurrences. The Olympic Project for Human Rights (OPHR), organized by black San Jose State sociology professor Harry Edwards, was a logical extension of the overall racial climate. Pointedly, Dr. Edwards said to his early critics, "The roots of the revolt of the black athlete spring from the same seed that produced the sit-ins, the freedom rides, and the rebellions in Watts, Detroit, and Newark . . ."[24]

On the opening day of classes at San Jose State in September 1967, a rally of seven hundred people resolved to disrupt the first game of the football season against the University of Texas at El Paso (UTEP) to protest racial discrimination. On October 7, Dr. Edwards formed the Olympic Committee for Human Rights (OCHR) in his home. It was decided that formal and organized protests were needed to redress the increasingly difficult conditions for black athletes. The OCHR formed the OPHR.

Six weeks later, at a strategy session in Los Angeles (on November 22 and 23), the participants—including activist James Foreman, Lew Alcindor (now Kareem Abdul-Jabbar), Lee Evans, Tommie Smith, and Otis Burrell—issued the following closing statement: "Black men and women athletes at a Black Youth Conference held in Los Angeles on the 23rd of November, 1967, have unanimously voted to fully endorse and participate in a boycott of the Olympic Games in 1968."[25]

Alcindor had been passionately eloquent in his remarks. He told the Conference, "Everybody knows me . . . last summer I was almost killed by a racist cop shooting at a black cat [man] in Harlem . . . Somewhere each of us has got to make a stand . . . I take my stand here."[26]

The statements were a direct challenge to the USOC and a clarion call to black athletes in all sports. After deciding to deliberately avoid the traditional civil rights groups like the National Urban League and the NAACP, a conference was held in the American Hotel in New York City on December 15, attended by Louis Lomax, Floyd McKissick, and Dr. Martin Luther King, Jr.

A list of demands were drawn up and directed to the USOC, the World Boxing Association, the World Boxing Council, the New York State Athletic Commission, and the New York Athletic Club. The demands were:

1. The restoration of Muhammad Ali's titles.
2. The removal of Avery Brundage as head of the USOC.
3. The continued exclusion of South African and Rhodesian teams from the United States and the Olympic Games.
4. The hiring of two additional black coaches to the Olympic track team—but not Stanley Wright.
5. The appointment of two blacks to the policymaking committee of the USOC.
6. The desegregation of the New York Athletic Club.

Muhammad Ali had been summarily stripped of his heavyweight title, and his fellow black athletes wanted justice done. Brundage was intensely disliked for his crass insensitivity to black problems and his hardline aversion to mixing politics and sport. Both South Africa and Rhodesia practiced official racial segregation at the time, and the committee deemed their continued athletic exclusion mandatory.

Stan Wright, who is black, had been appointed as an assistant coach for the 1968 United States squad but, he was, like Jesse Owens, considered at the time to be an "Uncle Tom." In answer to the demand concerning blacks on the USOC Executive Committee, Avery Brundage was quoted as replying, "I think there should be a qualified Negro on the USOC Board. I think Jesse Owens is a fine

boy and might make a good representative."
[sic][27]

The reaction to the OPHR's proposed boycott was loud and diverse. Black athletes
themselves were by no means totally supportive. Sample opinions provide clues to the
mood of the times. Among those in favor of
the boycott: Bill Gaines, a sprinter, said, "I'm
fully prepared to do anything necessary to
dramatize the plight of black people in this
country." Lee Evans noted that "There is need
for anything that brings about unity among
black people and points up the fact that successful blacks maintain their ties with the
black community." Ralph Boston declared
that "If we decide on some kind of protest, I'd
be less than a man not to participate. I'd be
letting myself down, my family, my race."[28]

In a dissenting opinion John Thomas said,
"How much pride can you lose by emerging
an Olympic champion?" Larry Livers, an AAU
hurdles champion, replied, "I would rather
see boycotts against domestic indoor and
outdoor meets. That's where the black is really exploited . . .I would support that kind of
boycotting." Willye White said, "I can't see
passing up the Olympics . . . I am an athlete."[29]

The New York Times' heralded white
sports columnist Red Smith declared that athletics have been "the Negro's best friend."
The great Jesse Owens was quoted as saying,
"I am not in accord with those who advocate
a boycott of the Olympic Games . . . athletics
help youngsters who do not have the money
to go on to colleges of their choice . . ."[30]

But Professor Charles Hamilton of Columbia University, the coauthor of *Black Power*
with Stokely Carmichael, declared, "The boycott is very necessary. It gives us another way
to confront the system."[31] An *Ebony* magazine
poll found only 1 percent of black athletes
agreeing with the boycott, 71 percent against
it, and 28 percent undecided. The OPHR

clearly lacked support among the rank and
file in early 1968.

An interim boycott against the New York
Athletic Club (which had no black members
and few, if any, Jewish ones) meet on February 15, 1968, was moderately successful. Led
by Catholic groups, the invited high school
teams withdrew; the service academies withdrew; and the Soviets canceled. That very
morning, newspapers had headlined the
readmittance of South Africa to the Olympic
Games by a secret ballot of seventy-one members at an IOC meeting in Grenoble, France.
South Africa had agreed to integrate its Olympic team, though it still planned to hold segregated Olympic trials. A three-man IOC del-
egation to South Africa that included an
African, had reported the reforms. However,
only nine black athletes crossed the picket
line at Madison Square Garden, where black
activist H. Rap Brown suggested the arena be
blown up. Intense emotion surrounded the
OPHR.

Said O. J. Simpson of the NYAC meet: "I
wouldn't run that weekend if my mother was
holding the meet." Harry Edwards angrily declared after hearing of South Africa's readmittance: "Let whitey run his own Olympics."[32]
Within two weeks of South Africa's readmittance, nearly all African nations and some
Third World nations withdrew from the 1968
Games.

The OPHR and the South African issue
effected the first major partnership between
the black athletes of Africa and America. It
also dramatized the gap between the first
generation of post-World War II black athletes
and their mid-sixties successors. During the
1967–68 academic year, black athletes at
thirty-seven predominantly white colleges
had raised demands for more black coaches,
faculty, trainers, and cheerleaders, and expressed sympathy with the OPHR.

Two months after the NYAC meet, UTEP
Track Coach Wayne Vandenburg summarily

dropped six blacks from his team (including Bob Beamon) for refusing to run against Brigham Young University (BYU). BYU was a Mormon institution which adhered to that religion's belief that blacks were damned by the Biblical curse of Ham. (The football coach at the University of Wyoming had done the same thing for the same reasons.) UTEP President Joseph Ray refused to rescind Vandenburg's dismissals. Racial tensions across the country were already near the boiling point because of Dr. Martin Luther King's assassination by a white man on April 4.

The next major national meet was the AAU championships. It was decided among the participating black athletes that if two-thirds of them agreed to boycott before the Olympic Trials were held, then the boycott was on. Just before the Trials in July, a meeting of approximately forty athletes was convened by Dr. Edwards at Pomona, California. During the previous week, the IOC had changed their position on South Africa and barred it from the Games. The growing attention paid to the proposed boycott and the euphoria over South Africa's expulsion, encouraged the black athletes to use the Trials for symbolic racial gestures of solidarity.

The USOC became aware of the proposed actions at the Trials at Pomona, and reacted by cancelling the victory ceremonies. Subsequently, the USOC stated that the Trials were not the real Trials and transferred these Olympic qualification events to Lake Tahoe, California—ostensibly for high altitude training for Mexico City's atmosphere at 7,349 feet. This sudden move appeared to be aimed more at the OPHR than for its practical benefits. Surely, blacks reasoned, the USOC could plan better than that.

Avery Brundage made matters worse when he was quoted as saying, "It seems a little ungrateful to attempt to boycott something which has given them [blacks] such great opportunities."[33]

At Tahoe, where the victory ceremonies were also cancelled, twelve blacks went on record as supporting the boycott and thirteen were against. Support for the OPHR had grown. Those who agreed to boycott were released from the group's pledge to "Do Your Own Thing." There would be no demonstrations at the Trials. The following month, on August 15, a National Conference on Black Power was held in Philadelphia, and there the OPHR became an integral part of the nation's black social revolution.

Within a year, a small but determined group of black athletes had succeeded in focusing the world's attention on their plight and that of black America. They arrived in Mexico City buoyed by the past year's experience, and left with a record total of twenty-seven Olympic medals in track and field—nineteen of them gold, and seventeen world records.

1968: The XIXth Olympiad at Mexico City, Mexico

This Olympiad is remembered principally for two events: Bob Beamon's new world record in the long jump and the victory stand demonstration by Tommie Smith and John Carlos. After all the meetings, caucusing, and reconsiderations, most black athletes were not sure what they were going to do as a form of protest. But they did know they were ready to perform.

On October 14, Jim Hines and Charles Greene (nursing a sore leg), finished first and third in the 100-meter dash. At the AAU Nationals that year, Hines from Texas Southern University, became the first man to clock a legal sub-ten-second reading for that event—9.9 in a semi-final heat. Greene attended the University of Nebraska and was a six-time NCAA Indoor and Outdoor 100-meter champion, and a four-time AAU Indoor and Outdoor winner in the century distance. According to Matthews, Hines refused to shake hands with Brundage during the medal ceremonies. Lee Evans and Tommie Smith watched from the stands.

Some black athletes were dissuaded from protesting by offers from sports companies. Vincent Matthews wrote that ". . . payments contributed to the reluctance of many to become totally committed in The Olympic Project for Human Rights."[34] Also, during a pre-Olympic stopover at Denver, Colorado, for outfitting and processing, the athletes agreed that a boycott was out of the question— though several proposals, such as the wearing of black arm bands and uniforms, were discussed.

On October 16, Smith and Carlos finished first and third in the 200-meter dash finals. While waiting under the stands for the awards ceremonies, Smith pulled two black gloves, purchased by his and Evans' wives, from his bag and gave the left glove to Carlos. On the spur of the moment they agreed on their gesture, which would be witnessed around the world and forever change the image of the black American athlete.

On the victory stand during the playing of America's National Anthem, Smith raised his right black-gloved fist high and straight above his head, and Carlos raised his left black-gloved fist as well. Smith wore a knotted black scarf around his neck and both wore long black socks and no shoes. Both stood with heads bowed, eyes closed, not saying a word. The deed was done.

What had prompted such courage in such a public forum? Smith was born in Acworth, Texas, on June 5, 1944; one of eight children of a migrant farm worker. He set four world records in 1966, in the 200-meters and 220-yard dash; a year later he set more world marks in the 400-meters and 440-yard dash. His world record at Mexico City was his seventh. In addition, he was AAU and NCAA 200/

220 champion in 1967, and AAU 200-meter champion in 1968.

His statement to WABC-TV's Howard Cosell, after the race, succinctly explained his feelings: "I wore a black right-hand glove and Carlos wore the left-hand glove of the same pair. My raised right hand stood for the power in black America. Carlos' raised left hand stood for the unity of black America. Together they formed an arch of unity and power. The black scarf around my neck stood for black pride. The black sock with no shoes stood for black poverty in racist America. The totality of our effort was the regaining of black dignity."[35]

John Carlos was born in New York City on June 5, 1945, and, after withdrawing from East Texas State because of racial discrimination, he enrolled at San Jose State. "In Harlem, you're not brought up to take what they do in Texas."[36] In his mind, nothing the USOC could do to him would be worse than what he had already experienced. His best ever performance was a nonratified clocking of 19.7 seconds in illegal spiked shoes for 200-meters, at the 1968 Olympic Trials. In 1969, he was AAU and NCAA champion at 200-meters and 220-yards, and equaled the world records in the 60-yard dash and the 100-yard dash.

Smith and Carlos were ejected from the Olympic Village by the IOC and subjected to vilification at home. Carlos said his "parents caught hell. They didn't really understand at the time. They seemed to be ashamed to be my parents."[37] (Carlos later played professional football and, at the 1984 Games, was named as a special assistant for the USOC.)

Lee Evans felt duty bound to do something since he and Smith were good friends. Their wives had bought the black gloves. Just before the 400-meter final, Evans, Larry James, and Ron Freeman were approached by a visibly nervous and shaking Douglas F. Roby, the USOC president, Stan Wright, and several other USOC officials. In a stammering voice, Roby warned against any demonstrations.

James screamed at Wright, "Listen, you better get this sonofabitch out of here, or I'll punch him in the mouth."[38]

On the victory stand in the rain afterwards, Evans, James, and Freeman, who finished first, second, and third, respectively, wore black berets and saluted. Evans' time of 43.86 seconds was a new world record.

While at San Jose State in 1968, Evans won the NCAA 440-yard title, five AAU titles, and was a member of the 1972 Olympic 1600-meter relay team. James attended Villanova and won the NCAA Indoor 440-yard title three straight years, and the Outdoor title in 1970. Though Freeman, of Arizona State, finished with a Bronze Medal he ran the fastest 440-meters on record—43.2 seconds—on the second leg of the 1600-meter relay.

After Matthews, Freeman, James, and Evans set a world record in the 1600-meter relay, they mounted the victory stand with their left hands under their jackets. After receiving their medals, they gave a salute and stood in a military at-ease position during the National Anthem. Matthews would perform in the 1972 Games, winning a second gold medal in the 400-meter run.

Rod Smith, Pender, Greene, and Hines set a world record in the 400-meter relay. At the 1968 AAU Nationals, both Smith, of San Jose State, and Hines shared a new world record of 9.9 seconds for 100-meters. Pender had made the Olympic finals of the 100-meters in 1964 and 1968, but placed sixth each time. A graduate of Adelphi University and later a career Army officer, he tied world Indoor marks in 1972 for 50-yards and 60-yards.

Davenport and Hall finished first and second in the 110-meter hurdles. Hall, from Villanova University, had set an Olympic record of 13.3 seconds in his first semifinal heat, but came in second in the final. Davenport, nicknamed "Cool Breeze," had made the 1964

team but never made the finals. He later competed on Olympic Teams in 1972, 1976, and was one of the first of two blacks in the Winter Olympics in 1980. As a student at Southern University he won the AAU Outdoor hurdles in 1965–67, and tied for first place in 1969. He was one of the greatest hurdlers ever.

The athletic event of the 1968 Olympiad and perhaps in all of recorded sports history was Bob Beamon's unparalleled performance in the long jump. Beamon had remained aloof from the OPHR events up until Mexico City, being one of the nine blacks to run in the NYAC meet in February because he wanted a free plane ticket home to New York. But in 1968, before coming to the Games, he had a string of twenty long jump wins in twenty-one meets. A few weeks before the NYAC meet, at the NAIA Indoors, Beamon set a world indoor record of 27 feet 1 inch. In March at the NCAA Indoors, he completed an historic double—winning both the long jump in a world record leap of 27 feet 2¾ inches, and two hours later the triple jump at 52 feet 3 inches.

On the day of his unprecedented feat, he was driven to the Estadio Olympico in a chauffeured limousine provided by a friend. While warming up he said to Ralph Boston, "I feel I can jump twenty-eight feet today." Charley Mays, the third American jumper, noticed Beamon's wife, Bertha, sitting in the stands. Totally relaxed, free of tension, and, as the fourth scheduled jumper, Beamon was content to watch his lesser talented Olympic colleagues. But it was beginning to cloud up and it looked like it would rain. At 3:36 P.M. his number, 254, was called, and all he wanted to do was get in a good leap before it rained. After removing his warm-ups he stood at the end of the long jump runway, 130 feet from the take-off board; nineteen strides from where he stood.

Beamon went through his own pre-jump check list, rehearsing the jump in his mind like an Army general planning an invasion.

Indeed, he meant to attack the take-off board. Of the track events, perhaps only the pole vault, the high jump, and the long jump lend themselves to large percentage increases in world marks, if all the right elements converge in perfect order. That day, Bob Beamon was in sync with the universe.

After Beamon's right foot perfectly pushed off the take-off board, ". . . he soared, his mind went blank, and his power of hearing, curiously, deserted him. The whole stadium went silent. His fists were clenched, his arms flung out for balance. He spread his knees and lifted them waist-high, his feet leading the way, his upper torso surprisingly erect."[39] Ralph Boston said, "I thought he would never come down."[40]

Beamon's first thought was that the jump felt good, perhaps more than 27 feet 6 inches. He then had to wait longer than normal for an official measurement; the marshalls quickly discovered that his jump was so long that their optical equipment was not designed to measure that great a distance. The outer limit was 28 feet, even in Mexico City's rarified air. After getting a new tape, the officials measured Beamon's distance—8.9 meters or 29 feet 2½ inches. But no, that was not humanly possible. A different set of officials measured it again. The result was the same. Twenty-nine feet, two and one-half inches. The most superlative accomplishment in the history of recorded sports.

In a daze, Beamon's mind was like a jammed switchboard, overloaded and temporarily unable to fully comprehend reality. Anxiously, he said to Boston, "What do I do now? I know you're gonna kick my ass." But Boston, called "the Master" by Beamon, knew it was all over for everybody else; he had just witnessed a once-in-a-millennium event from front and center. Beamon had exceeded the World Record by *almost two feet!* "No, no" said the Master, "I can't jump that far." The Russian jumper, Igor Ter-Ovanesyan dryly in-

toned, "After that jump, the rest of us are children."[41]

Within minutes, Beamon's brain sorted out reality from illusion, the present from that somnambulant state induced by his effort. It had all seemed so easy, so effortless; there was no strain. Without knowing it and with no sense of embarrassment or chagrin, he sank to his knees and covered his face with his hands, his heart pounding. "Tell me I'm not dreaming. It's not possible. I can't believe it. Tell me I'm not dreaming." And then it started to rain. Later, Beamon with black socks on in a show of support for Smith and Carlos, tried a second jump and went 26 feet 4½ inches. Boston won the bronze medal.

Edward Caruthers, a 1967 Pan-Am Games high jump gold medalist from Arizona State, posted a personal best of 7 feet 3½ inches, but had to settle for a silver medal behind Dick Fosbury, whose jumping style was later termed "the Fosbury flop."

The black women Olympians were no less brilliant at Mexico City. Wyomia Tyus became the second black female to win more than one gold medal in a single Olympiad, and the first to set world records in two events. She repeated as gold medalist in the 100-meters. She finished her Olympic career with three golds and one silver medal.

Barbara Ferrell, Margaret Bailes, and Mildrette Netter were Tyus' relay mates in the 400-meter relay. Ferrell, of Los Angeles State and the L.A. Mercurettes, won the Pan-Am Games 100-meters in 1967, and qualified for the U.S. Olympic Team in 1972, but did not win a medal. Bailes, of the Oregon Track Club, was only seventeen at the time. She was the 1968 AAU 100-meter champion and twice equaled the world record of 11.1 seconds. Netter attended Alcorn A & M and was on the 1972 Olympic 400-meter relay team.

Madeline Manning's career was among the longest—nearly fifteen years. From Tennessee State, she was a six-time AAU winner at 800-meters, a Pan-Am Games winner, a World University Games winner in 1966, and an Olympic silver medalist in 1972. She would have been a contender in 1980, if President Jimmy Carter had not forced a U.S.-led boycott at Moscow. Manning was easily the best female 800-meter runner the United States had ever produced. She became an ordained minister shortly after retiring from racing.

Although the OPHR did not effect a boycott of the 1968 Games, it furnished startling evidence that the American athletic community could no longer take black athletes for granted. Changes were made as a result of the OPHR effort and other protest movements with similar aims. Conferences were held from coast to coast to consider the hiring of more black staff members. The Pan-African Games, organized by Dr. Leroy Walker in 1971 at Duke University, saw black athletes from Africa and America participating; the black American team won, 117–78.

But as Abraham Ordia, president of the Supreme Council For Support In Africa, jokingly said of the Pan-African Games, "There is no way Africa can lose this meet. Why? Because the best athletes on America's teams also come from Africa."[42]

Two other results from the Mexico City Games are noteworthy. Jesse Owens wrote another book entitled, *I Have Changed*, in which he sought to let people know that his beliefs on some issues had altered and that he saw a need for more direct action on racial matters. Though some earlier critics scoffed at this change of heart as being too late, others welcomed his metamorphosis.

As Vince Matthews pointed out, most team members at Mexico City considered Owens to be ". . . a messenger sent by the USOD to determine the mood of black athletes."[43] Owens had been publicly rebuffed at a meeting of black and white athletes on the night following Tommie Smith's and John Carlos' demonstration. Some were even more hostile.

Said Willye White: "I live in the same town as Jesse Owens, Chicago. We're both black athletes, but the only time I ever see Jesse Owens is at the Olympics every four years."[44]

Another item of interest was an announcement by Kenneth Pitzer, the president of Stanford University. In November 1969, Pitzer announced that Stanford would henceforth honor what he called an athlete's "Right of Conscience." This Right would allow the athlete to boycott an event which he or she had deemed personally repugnant. Though it was not heartily endorsed by other schools, it was nevertheless a breakthrough.

1972: The XXth Olympiad at Munich, West Germany

While the Mexico City Olympics were remembered in part for the victory stand demonstrations by Tommie Smith and John Carlos, the Munich Olympics are remembered for the massacre of eleven Israeli Olympians by their Palestinian kidnappers and a record seven gold medals in swimming won by Mark Spitz. It was not an especially memorable Olympics for black Americans.

Seven gold medals were earned and two world records were set. The medalists are listed in the Reference section.

Vincent Matthews came back from the 1968 Games to win his second gold medal. Rod Milburn was simply brilliant at Munich where automatic timing to hundredths of a second was used for the first time. His time of 13.24 seconds in the 110-meter hurdles set Olympic and world records. He was a three-time AAU champion, a two-time NCAA winner, and Pan-Am winner in 1971. Like his predecessor, Willie Davenport, he matriculated at Southern University.

Randy Williams became the youngest Olympic long jump winner at nineteen. He won the silver medal in Montreal in 1976 and qualified for the team in 1980. From the University of Southern California, he was NCAA titleholder in 1972 and AAU winner in 1972–73.

Black, Taylor, Tinker, and Hart sound like the name of a law firm, but these four runners set a new world record in the 400-meter relay. Black, from North Carolina Central, won two medals. He was NCAA, NCAA-College Division, and NAIA champion in 1971. Taylor just missed edging out Valeri Borzov in the 100-meter final where he was the only American finalist. (Eddie Hart and Rey Robinson failed to make it to the starting line in time for their heats.) A Texas Southern student, Taylor was AAU 100-meter champion in 1972. Tinker went to Kent State and ran the third leg on the 400-meter team.

Eddie Hart, running for the University of California at Berkeley, and Rey Robinson had qualified in their first heat, but failed to show up in time for the second heat and were disqualified. Like Howard Porter Drew in 1912, Harrison Dillard in 1948, and Ray Norton in 1960, Hart was considered almost a sure winner. At the Finals Trials he had equaled the world record of 9.9 seconds for 100-meters. In addition he was NCAA 100-yard dash winner in 1970.

Hart and Robinson thought their heats were scheduled after the 10,000-meter heat, but they were really scheduled earlier. The USOC had posted one set of schedules but the coaches had another set of times. The Games officials allowed no exceptions.

Arnie Rey Robinson, whose real first names were Clarence Earl, attended San Diego State and was a NCAA winner in 1970. He was the Pan-Am titleholder in 1971, and his six AAU titles is matched only by William DeHart Hubbard and Ralph Boston. Winning a bronze medal in 1972 in the long jump, he roared back at Montreal four years later to take the gold.

Wayne Collett of UCLA finished second behind Matthews in the 400-meter run,

though he had won the Trials event. During the anthem ceremony, Matthews stood casually with his warm-ups undone, and was pointedly uninterested in respecting the American flag. Collett stood next to Matthews on top and appeared even more deliberately disrespectful throughout the playing of the anthem. For this behavior they were banned for life by the IOC. The massacre of the Israeli athletes was thus not the only tense moment at Munich, although it certainly seemed the darkest day in Olympic history.

By the 1972 Olympiad, black male athletes were much more assertive and less willing to obey orders. They were world class athletes and each had his own way of training, which frequently clashed with opinions of head coach Bill Bowerman. Luckily, the black assistant coach, Hoover Wright of Prairie View College, was helpful.

There was even a possibility that another boycott attempt would be made, because the IOC had allowed the Rhodesian team to participate under the flag of Great Britain. With his experience at Mexico City in his mind, Matthews persuaded John Smith, Lee Evans, Wayne Collett, and Chuck Smith to issue the following statement in solidarity with Ethiopia and Kenya, which were threatening to pull out:

> In the light of the Rhodesian acceptance into the Games, the United States black athletes now in Olympic Park believe it imperative to take a stand concerning the issue. We denounce Rhodesia's participation and if they are allowed to compete, we will take a united stand with our African brothers.

Later, the IOC changed its policy and banned the Rhodesian squad which, it was then found out, had black athletes. Thus the statement, written by Chuck Smith, referred to a moot issue but the point was nonetheless made.

When Matthews and Collett came off the victory stand, they knew that life would never be the same. Matthews' mother was crying and his fiancée was angry. Collett, from a solidly middle class family, was engaged to be married in two weeks and his family back in California was stunned.

Matthews' motives stemmed in part from America's institutionalized racism, and in part from his lack of satisfaction from his weaker Mexico City protest. Correspondingly, Collett was loud and clear, saying to ABC's Howard Cosell, "I didn't stand at attention on the victory stand because I couldn't do it with a clear conscience .. . I feel that, looking back on it now, my actions on the victory stand probably will mirror the attitude of white America toward blacks—total, casual as long as we're not embarrassing them."[45]

For their actions, Avery Brundage sent the following letter to Stan Buck, the USOC president:

Dear Mr. Buck,

The whole world saw the disgusting display of your two athletes, when they received their gold and silver medals for the 400 m. event yesterday.

This is the second time the USOC has permitted such occurrences on the athletic field. It is the Executive Board's opinion that these two athletes have broken rule 26, paragraph 1 in respect of the traditional Olympic spirit and ethic and are, therefore, eliminated from taking part in any future Olympic competition.

Yours sincerely,
Avery Brundage

Matthews eventually secured a job as a payroll coordinator for a youth project and Collett became a lawyer. While the bannings at Munich did not get the same international exposure as the demonstrations at Mexico City, they were still grave evidence of the black distrust felt toward USOC authorities, and the residual resentment toward white America by black youth.

Mable Ferguson, Cheryl Toussaint, and Madeline Manning shared their silver medal victory with Kathy Hammond, a white runner. Ferguson was only seventeen at the time, but she had already won the AAU 400-meter title in 1971, and in 1973 she added National titles in the 400-yard and the 220-yard dashes.

Toussaint was outstanding at the 400/440 and 800/880 distances. A New York University graduate and a product of Fred Thompson's Atoms Track Club in Brooklyn, New York, she won the Nationals title at 880 yards in 1970–73 but was eliminated in the heats at Munich. She also held the world record in the Indoor 600-yard dash. Another of Thompson's athletes, Gail Fitzgerald, competed in the Pentathlon in 1972 and 1976 but did not win a medal.

1976: The XXIst Olympiad at Montreal, Canada

The Olympics at Montreal coincided with the 40th anniversary of the 1936 Games at Berlin. The United States had fought in three major wars—World War II, Korea, and Vietnam—since then. The Supreme Court had integrated the nation's public schools, more facilities had been built, and the coaching and competition was vastly improved. How much progress had been made on the track?

Black athletes continued to dominate the sprinting and jumping events but the results were uneven. Since 1936, thirty-nine men had either set or equaled the world record in the 100-meter dash—twenty-five of them black Americans. The record in 1936 was set by Jesse Owens at 10.2 seconds with hand-held timing; by 1976, it was 9.9 seconds. Owens had once said of a sub-ten-second time, "They'll never do it . . . Mathematics will bear me out."[46] Jim Hines ran a 9.9 second, 100-meter dash on July 10, 1968.

In the 200-meters, Owens also had the 1936 world record at 20.7 seconds but in 1976 the record was 19.8 seconds, set by Don Quarrie (of Jamaica) who was also black. During that forty-year period, twenty men equaled or set new world records at this distance—twelve of them black Americans. But significantly, all the world record holders in the 100-meters, the 200-meters, and the 400-meters from 1968 through 1984 were black.

The figures seem to add weight to theories that sprinters are "born" but the longer sprints require more than natural ability. The fact that so many blacks are sprint record holders does not mean that blacks are better natural sprinters; but that more athletically inclined blacks took an active interest in sprinting than did the general white population.

(In 1972, Dr. Delano Merriwether, a physician who was the first black medical student at Duke University Medical School, ran the 100-yard dash in 9 seconds. He had never run before 1970, and he never trained.)

In 1936, Archie Williams, a black quarter-miler, had the 400-meters world record at 46.1 seconds; and by 1976 the record was down to 43.8 seconds—set by Lee Evans. In 1967, Tommie Smith became the only man ever to hold the world record at both 200-meters and 400-meters, an astounding accomplishment.

The first black female world record holder in the 100-meters or 200-meters was Wilma Rudolph in 1960, at 11.3 seconds and 22.9 seconds, respectively. Only two other black runners, Wyomia Tyus and Barbara Ferrell, either set new records or tied existing records in the 100-meters. Rudolph stands alone as the only black world record setter in the 200-meters.

Ten of the record setters in the long jump are black Americans, and the record was raised from 26-feet 8-inches in 1936 to Bob Beamon's phenomenal 29 feet 2½-inch leap in Mexico City in 1968. In the high jump, six of the first sixteen record holders were black—John Thomas was the last one in 1960.

While the men's track teams at black colleges had, by 1976, won NAIA and NCAA Division II titles, the women finally broke through two years after the Munich Olympics, when Prairie View A & M College in Texas won the AIAW title. Coached by Barbara Jacket, this team won the Outdoor title and repeated in 1976. The country was just beginning to catch up in women's athletics, due in large measure to the passage of Title IX of the Education Amendments Act passed by Congress in 1972.

But as much progress as was made in the United States, the rest of the world—Eastern Europe in particular—made even more with their ultra-scientific approach to all track and field events. In the 1976 Olympic Games in Montreal, no black Americans won gold medals in any individual sprinting events. The medalists are listed in the Reference section.

The star of this Olympiad was Edwin Moses, a physics major from Morehouse College. He was born in Dayton, Ohio, on August 31, 1955. Few track experts realized that he would dominate his event (the 400-meter hurdles) as no other athlete had ever done before. Moses constantly spoke of the lessons in life learned at Morehouse, a black all-male college in Atlanta. He noted, "At Morehouse, we learned to do without, and we had to make adjustments and sacrifices. But we were highly motivated."[47]

Moses set a new 400-meter hurdles world record (47.6 seconds) on July 25, 1976, in Montreal and gradually lowered it to 47.02 seconds on August 31, 1983. In the 1984 Games at Los Angeles, Moses, who was among the most highly respected athletes of his era, was accorded the honor of giving the Athlete's Oath.

Millard Hampton, from UCLA, had won the 200-meter Olympic Trials in 20.10 seconds, but settled for second place at Montreal. Hampton's 400-meter relay mates, Steve Riddick, John Jones, and Harvey Glance were among the world's best sprinters in the mid-'70s. Riddick, of Norfolk State, reached the semifinals of the 100-meter competition at Montreal; Jones attended the University of Texas and went on to a professional football career with the New York Jets; and Glance won the 1976 NCAA 100-yard and 220-yard dashes. Glance, of Auburn, won the NCAA 100-yard title again in 1977.

Herman Frazier, Maxie Parks, Benny Brown, and Fred Newhouse won the 1600-meter gold medal but did not set any records. Frazier attended Arizona State and won the NCAA 440-yard dash in 1977, and tried to make the United States Winter Olympic team in 1980 as a bobsledder. Parks, of UCLA, was an AAU champion in 1976. Brown, also of UCLA, earned his relay spot by finishing fourth in the Trials. Newhouse, from Prairie View A&M, should have made the 1972 team, but made up for it with two medals in 1976. His third-leg time was 43.8 seconds.

James Butts, from UCLA, was NCAA triple jump champion in 1972. Like Newhouse, Butts just missed making the team in 1972. Dwayne Evans attended the University of Arizona and also won the 1979 AAU 200-meter title.

Dr. Leroy Walker of North Carolina Central University was named head coach for the men's team at Montreal, and former Olympian Lee Calhoun was one of his assistants.

Debra Sapenter, Sheila Ingram, Pam Jiles, and Rosalyn Bryant all won silver medals in the 1600-meter relay. The United States did not win a gold medal in this event until 1984. Sapenter, from Prairie View A&M, won AAU titles in 1974–75; Ingram set a new American record of 51.31 seconds for 400-meters at Montreal in the quarterfinals but lost it hours later to Sapenter. (She set a new record of 50.90 seconds in the semifinals but lost that one minute later to Bryant who ran a 50.62 clocking.) Jiles, of Dillard University and LSU, was a better 200-meter runner and was the 1975 Pan-Am Games 100-meter champion.

Rosalyn Bryant was from Chicago, and attended Long Beach State. She was easily one of the best sprinters in the late '70s. Her anchor leg time in the 1600-meter final of 49.7 seconds assured the silver medal. She was also AAU Indoor title holder in 1975 and 1977.

Dr. Evie Dennis scored a victory of sorts in 1976, by becoming the first black woman officer of the USOC.

Amidst the 1976 Games was an African boycott by thirty countries over New Zealand's presence. New Zealand had entertained a rugby team from racist South Africa earlier in the year and, to protest New Zealand's action, the Supreme Council for Sport in Africa called for a mass withdrawal. Black American athletes were not pressured by African Olympic officials to participate, though many sympathized with this protest. The world was thus deprived of a potential world record 1500-meter race between Filbert Bayi of Tanzania and John Walker of New Zealand.

Walker had set a new mile record of 3:49.4 minutes the year before. In 1973, Reggie McAffee had become the first black American to run a mile under four minutes. The distance races, in particular the mile and the marathon, had become more popular than the sprints, since the running craze matured in the United States.

In other developments, the IOC began allowing athletes to receive regular salaries from sports firms in 1974, as long as the monies were paid to national associations or bona fide clubs in good standing with the International Amateur Athletic Federation (IAAF). This certainly rid the sport of some of the on-going under-the-table payments to athletes. In a profound, though unrelated matter, the Canadian Olympic officials left their government with a debt of roughly one billion dollars.

The United States was forced to withdraw from the 1980 Moscow Olympics by President Jimmy Carter, because of the Soviet Union's invasion of Afghanistan in 1979. Japan, West Germany, and Canada also withdrew as a measure of protest. Though many decried the intrusion of politics into the Games, in reality, the Games had been used as political footballs since 1900. Black American athletes expressed only lukewarm or no support for President Carter's actions.

Two years before, Congress passed the Amateur Sports Act which empowered the USOC to coordinate America's efforts in the Games and appropriated $16 million to fund the effort. The fielding of superior Olympic teams had by then become an everyday preoccupation of the USOC, and the increased attention paid off at the 1984 Games at Los Angeles, even though the Soviet Union and its allies boycotted in retaliation for President Carter's action in 1980.

1984: The XXIIIrd Olympiad at Los Angeles, California

World record performances had slowed down in the eight years since America's last Olympic appearance in 1976. No new men's records were set in the 100-meters, 200-meters, 400-meters, long jump, or triple jump. Renaldo Nehemiah, a black American hurdler, finally cracked the thirteen-second barrier in the 110-meter hurdles in August 1981, with a time of 12.93 seconds. The women, however, lowered the 100-meter mark from 10.88 seconds to 10.79 seconds and the 200-meter mark from 22.06 seconds to 21.71 seconds. American companies like Colgate-Palmolive began sponsoring women's track meets and

participation jumped considerably. But women did not cash in heavily with endorsements, or in fees paid by meet promoters.

The United States team for the Los Angeles Games was one of the most talented ever seen, and of the fifty-seven American medals won in track and field forty-one were won by blacks. The black medalists are listed in the Reference section.

Carl Lewis was unquestionably the star of this Olympiad. He received more pre-Olympic publicity than any athlete had ever experienced before, and he lived up to expectations. Lewis, born in New Jersey and a student at the University of Houston, did not set any individual world records, but he did set a new Olympic record in the 200-meter dash finals. He won the 100-meter dash by 89 feet, the largest margin ever. His winning long jump distance of 28 feet and ¼ inch, was achieved on his first leap. By 1984, only four men had ever jumped over 28 feet and only Bob Beamon and Lewis had jumped over 28 feet, 6 inches.

Lewis, a flashy and supremely confident performer, was criticized for not attempting a longer distance in the long jump, even though no one came within a foot of his initial jump. Brooks Johnson, the black head coach of the men's team, did not press Lewis or try to change his mind.

Lewis was the first Olympic performer since Jesse Owens in 1936, to win four track and field gold medals in one Olympiad.

Sam Graddy, from the University of Tennessee, was part of the 400-meter relay team with Emmit King, Willie Gault, and Carl Lewis, who set the world record in Helsinki in August 1983 in 37.86 seconds. Along with Ron Brown, Calvin Smith, and Carl Lewis, Graddy helped set another world record in the Olympic 400-meter relay in 37.83 seconds. The second place Jamaican team was 79/100ths of a second behind. The Lewis-Baptiste-Jefferson sweep in the 100-meters was the first such all-United States victory since 1912.

Babers spent his early life in West Germany where his father was stationed in the Air Force. McKay was a Georgia Tech freshman who had won the NCAA Indoor and Outdoor 440-yard titles. In the 110-meter hurdles, Foster, from UCLA, was favored but was edged out by Kingdom in the finals.

Edwin Moses, almost twenty-nine, picked up where he left off at the 1976 Games. He held the world record for the 400-meter hurdles and won the Olympic event by a margin of 38/100ths of a second over Danny Harris. Before the final in Los Angeles Moses had an unbeaten streak of 102 races, eighty-nine of them in the finals. By the end of the year, Moses had extended his unbeaten streak in his specialty to over 105 races, the longest by any track athlete in any event. Of the ten best times in his event, nine of them belonged to him.

Al Joyner won the triple jump over Mike Conley by a margin of only 8/100ths of a meter. When his sister, Jackie, won her silver medal on August 4, she and Al became the first brother-sister track and field medal winners on the same day. Al, nicknamed "Sweetwater," attended Arkansas State. At 6-feet 1 inch, 168 pounds, he was considered a stringbean. Conley, of the University of Arkansas, as the 1984 NCAA triple jump champion.

Earl Jones' bronze medal in the 800-meter run was the first medal by a black American at that distance since 1952.

The black female Olympians were brilliant. Of twenty-four total medals won by American women, eighteen were by blacks. Valerie Brisco-Hooks joined the select company of Wilma Rudolph and Wyomia Tyus as a triple gold medal winner. She set new Olympic records in the finals of both the 200-meter and 400-meter dash.

As a triple winner, Brisco-Hooks had reason to expect endorsements of the type previous multiple winners had enjoyed from the corporate world. The response to her, however, was initially lukewarm but heightened considerably ten months after the Games. Mary Lou Retton, who is white and who won a single gold medal in the gymnastics competition, was the prime recipient of corporate attention. The black press duly noted this discrepancy which only served to reinforce the black community's basic distrust of corporate America.

Evelyn Ashford, a UCLA graduate, might have been a triple winner but she settled for first place in the 100-meters and as anchor on the 400-meter relay team. Historically, Ashford had been very reclusive and rarely gave interviews or talked with opponents. But in Los Angeles she was more engaging and, having lost chances at the 1980 Games, was determined to come in a winner. Alice Brown's second place finish came just 3/100ths of a second ahead of Merlene Ottey-Page of Jamaica.

Benita Fitzgerald-Brown won the 100-meter hurdles over Shirley Strong of Great Britain—by 4/100ths of a second. Kim Turner was 18/100ths of a second behind Strong. In the 400-meter hurdles final, Judi Brown desperately tried to sprint to the finish but missed winning by 59/100ths of a second.

Alice Brown partly atoned for her silver medal in the 100-meter dash by helping Jeanette Bolden, Chandra Cheeseborough, and Evelyn Ashford win the gold in the 400-meter relay. Cheeseborough later added a third medal to her second place one in the 400-meter dash with a gold medal finish in the 400-meter relay. Along with Brisco-Hooks, Sherri Howard, and Lillie Leatherwood, Cheeseborough helped set a new Olympic record in the 1600-meter relay final. Leatherwood and Howard were joined by Diane Dixon and Denean Howard in winning the first heat to put them into the finals. Dixon and Denean Howard were then replaced by

Brisco-Hooks and Cheeseborough in the final, and this latter foursome set the new Olympic record. (Dixon once failed gym class at Brooklyn's Tech High, but was encouraged by Fred Thompson of the Atoms Track Club who told her she had Olympic potential.) It was the first Olympic record set by American women in this event.

Jackie Joyner (now Jackie Joyner-Kersee) was unable to match her performance in the Trials where she scored an American record of 6,520 points in the heptathlon. That would have been good enough for a gold medal at Los Angeles. Her Olympic score of 6,385 points was 5 points shy of Glynis Nunn's effort of 6,390. Bob Kersee, the black head coach at UCLA (now Joyner's husband), says Joyner is the best female athlete he has ever seen. Joyner is a solid 5-foot 10-inch, 145-pound athlete, who says basketball is her favorite sport.

There were many other black Olympic hopefuls who did not win medals but nevertheless are outstanding performers. Sydney Maree, a naturalized American born in South Africa, was injured and missed the 1500-meter run competition. David Patrick and Andre Phillips missed in the 400-meter hurdles; Larry Myricks and Tyke Peacock in the high jump; Jason Grimes in the long jump; Tony Banks in the 400-meter dash; David Mack in the 800-meter run and the 1500-meters; David Robinson and Johnny Gray in the 800-meters; and the veteran Rod Milburn in the 110-meter hurdles.

Among the women, Carl Lewis' sister, Carol, and Jodi Anderson missed in the long jump. Lewis has, at 22 feet 10-¾ inches, the second best jump ever for an American. Anderson holds the American record in this event at 23 feet and was a heptathlon competitor as well. Delisa Floyd, wife of former sprinter, Stanley Floyd, had become a mother and was unable to perform.

Other world class female athletes who either failed to make the team or missed capturing a medal included Dianne Williams in the 100-meter dash; LaShon Nedd and Rosalyn Bryant in the 400-meters; Robin Campbell in the 800-meters, and Missy Gerald in the 100-meter hurdles.

Female athletes had come a long way since before World War II. Nell Jackson tells of feeling two separate attitudes toward women. Outside the Tuskegee community, ". . . there was a stigma against women participating in sports; that it was unfeminine, unladylike."[48] But there was no such stigma at Tuskegee in the late '30s and early '40s. Furthermore, Jackson believes that "Sports helped to break the [racial] ice in the South. We went to meets in Oklahoma and Texas where all the athletes were housed in community gyms and Army bases."[49] By 1984, racial restrictions seemed gone and the social stigma had disappeared, but the best black female performers were still concentrated in black colleges; selected clubs in New York City, Philadelphia, Chicago, and Los Angeles; and at predominantly white colleges on the West Coast. Ahead of tennis and basketball, track was the primary outlet for aspiring black American female athletes.

1988: The XXIVth Olympiad at Seoul, Korea

This Olympiad was marked by a major scandal in the men's 100-meters and several stirring performances by a fabulous female sprinter nicknamed Flo-Jo.

Ben Johnson, a Jamaican, who moved to Ontario, Canada, when he was 14, arrived in Seoul determined to outkick nemesis Carl Lewis, the 1984 100-meter gold medalist.

Lewis defeated Johnson seven consecutive times in 1985, but then lost five consecutive races—including the 1987 World Championships in Rome—to the man appropriately nicknamed Big Ben. Johnson claimed the

Rome title with a 9.83 effort, knocking a full tenth of a second off the world record.

Johnson was hobbled by (hamstring) injuries in February and May before the games. Lewis gave himself a major pre-Olympic confidence boost a month before the Seoul Games by winning in Zurich, Switzerland in 9.93 seconds. Calvin Smith was second (9.97) and Johnson was third (10.00).

Lewis' Zurich victory, combined with Johnson's physical problems, established Lewis as a heavy favorite to become the first male sprinter to retain an Olympic title. But when the starter's pistol for the 100-meter final exploded, so did Big Ben. Johnson never relinquished the lead and bolted past the finishing line in an astounding time of 9.79 seconds.

Canada went wild about Johnson's record-shattering achievement, but the celebration was short-lived. Three days after the race, Olympic officials announced that Johnson had failed a drug test (steroids), and the gold medal went to Lewis.

Johnson first denied that he had been taking anabolic steroids. But in June 1989, testifying before the Dubin Commission, he admitted he had used steroids throughout his career. Johnson, the 39th Olympic athlete to be disqualified because of drugs since testing began in 1968, was suspended for two years. The IAAF also took his 1987 Rome title even though he had passed the drug test in Rome.

Johnson's embarrassment proved to be a blessing for Lewis. At his father's funeral in May 1987, Lewis had placed his 1984 100-meter gold medal in his father's hands. He assured his mother that he would win another 100-meter gold.

Johnson's startling dash seemingly ended Lewis' dream. But he handled his disappointment with class, shaking Johnson's hand and congratulating him on his victory. Though Lewis had believed before the Games that Johnson was using steroids, he made no accusations. He didn't gloat when Johnson was stripped of his gold.

"I feel bad because the Canadian people were very supportive of him," Lewis said in *USA Today*, September 28, 1988. "He was a true hero to them and now that seems to have been taken away. I also feel bad for Ben because the whole world is looking at him and practically every place he goes, people are going to point their fingers and say he's a druggie."

Lewis, who won four gold medals at the 1984 Games, won gold in the 100-meters and the long jump. He added a silver medal in the 200-meters. Butch Reynolds set a world record (43.86) in the 400-meters.

On the women's side, Florence Griffith-Joyner of Los Angeles arrived in Seoul eager to display an array of physical talent that proved as dazzling as her outfits. The seventh of 11 children, Griffith-Joyner discovered she had the gift of speed when she was seven. She moved closer to fulfilling her destiny after marrying Al Joyner, the 1984 triple jump gold medalist.

Griffith-Joyner prepared for Seoul by studying Ben Johnson's explosive starts, analyzing Carl Lewis' form and adding definition to her body through a weight training program. She won the 100-meter in an Olympic record of 10.54 and took the 200-meter in 21.34, setting a new world record. She ran the third leg in the USA's victorious 4x100-meter relay effort and anchored the USA's 4-x400-meter team that won a silver medal.

Her Olympic success led to a flood of lucrative endorsement opportunities.

"Even I was surprised by the number of approaches by substantial companies," she said. "Everything from high tech electronics to Florence Griffith-Joyner dolls."

But in light of Johnson's disqualification for drug use, similar suspicions were raised because of Griffith-Joyner's quick physical development.

Responding to the accusations, she said, "Even when I was a little girl, people used to laugh at me and criticize me. I learned sticks and stones. . . ."

Her husband, Al, added: "We didn't let anything interrupt our dream. If an athlete's mental toughness breaks, that's it. All of this brought us together."

Griffith-Joyner was named winner of the Sullivan Award in March 1989, a month after she retired.

Al Joyner's sister, Jackie Joyner-Kersee, also won two gold medals—the heptathlon with a world record 7,291 point effort and the long jump with an Olympic record leap of 24-feet, 3¼ inches. Leading up to the Seoul Games, Joyner-Kersee, married to Olympic track coach Bob Kersee, won nine consecutive heptathlon events after capturing a silver medal in the event at the 1984 Games.

Black sprinters, led by Lewis and Griffith-Joyner, again claimed most of the medals in the spring events in Olympic competition.

1992: The XXVth Olympiad at Barcelona, Spain

The USA's Dream Team, featuring Magic, Michael, and other marquee names of the NBA, was the undisputed superstar of the Barcelona Games. (See Basketball section.)

A bevy of colorful costars, however, included Carl Lewis, Ben Johnson, and Jackie Joyner-Kersee and a host of emerging super athletes named Gail Devers, Gwen Torrence, Michael Johnson, and Mike Powell.

Powell drew large crowds to the long jump event, mainly because of his Herculean leap of 29-feet, 4½ inches at the '91 World Championships. Powell's jump ended Lewis' 65-meet winning streak and surpassed Bob Bemon's 1968 world record mark by two inches.

Powell fell short in Barcelona, finishing second to Lewis, who claimed the gold with a jump of 28-feet, 5½ inches. Powell jumped 28-feet, 4½ inches.

Said Powell: "I just didn't have it. Normally, I'm very exitable, up for the competition. My body felt flat." (*USA Today*, August 7, 1992.)

Michael Johnson, who in 1990 and 1991 became the only man to rank No. 1 in both the 200-meters and 400-meters, also fell flat in his Olympic effort. Weakened by food poisoning, Johnson failed to make the 200-meter final, but received a gold medal in the 4x100-meters. Great Britain's Linford Christie won the 100-meters, as Ben Johnson, disqualified for steroid use in Seoul, was eliminated in the semifinals.

Mike Marsh won the 200-meter gold in an Olympic record time of 43.5; Quincy Watts snatched the 400-meters and Kevin Young won the 400-meter hurdles. Carl Lewis won gold medals in the long jump and the 4x100-meters, pushing his gold count to eight. He also won a silver medal.

In the women's competition, Gail Devers became a crowd and world favorite winning the 100-meters and seemed on the verge of winning a second gold in the 100-meters hurdles, but fell after hitting the final hurdle.

Gwen Torrence took the 200-meters, but 30-year-old Jackie Joyner-Kersee stirred the emotions by winning a second consecutive heptathlon victory. Joyner-Kersee became the first woman to win two Olympic gold medals in multi-event competition.

Said Joyner-Kersee: "Because it was so historic, I really wanted to get the gold. It was a feeling of joy and relief when I came across the finish line." (*USA Today*, August 7, 1992.)

The American men's track team, won 20 medals overall, including eight golds; the U.S. women's track team won 10 medals, including four golds.

The Black Colleges

At the end of World War II, the major black college conferences were the Central Intercollegiate Athletic Association (CIAA), the Southeastern Athletic Conference (SEAC), and the Southwest Athletic Conference (SWAC). By the end of 1984, there were six black major conferences including one for unaffiliated schools. While it was difficult to qualify for participation in the NCAA events, the NAIA, which began including track and field in 1952, gave black schools an entry into world competition. It was a godsend for hundreds of black athletes who did not attend the large NCAA-affiliated institutions.

Seven years after the NAIA began track competition, Winston-Salem State Teacher's College, coached by Wilbur Ross, won the Outdoor title—the first national title won by a black school outside the traditional group of historically black colleges. In 1974, Prairie View A&M, coached by Barbara Jacket, won the AIAW title—the first national title by a black college women's team. (The complete list of national titles won by black colleges is listed in the Reference section.)

Jackson State, coached by Martin Epps, won the 1978 AIAW Women's Cross Country title.

The list of championships represents an astounding record amassed in such a short time. Few black schools have large student body populations, which makes their productivity even more amazing. Since track is the only major school sport with an international following, school administrators feel that outstanding teams are worth the expense in favorable publicity alone.

The Black College Coach

The profile of the successful black coach was outlined by the approach taken by Cleveland Abbott, Tuskegee's innovative leader in the mid-1920s. At that time, nearly all black coaches were teachers as well. Ed Hurt, who coached at Morgan State for forty years, was the head coach for football, basketball, base-

ball, and track. He was not alone in this regard. Other pioneers in track included William Bennett at Virginia State University, Nell Jackson at Tuskegee, George Wright and Al Priestly at Xavier, Wilbur Ross at Winston-Salem and Maryland Eastern Shore, Ed Temple at Tennessee State, Dr. Leroy Walker at North Carolina Central, and Stan Wright at Texas Southern.

SUMMARY

The foot race is probably mankind's oldest nonviolent form of athletic competition. Recorded history is replete with mention of these contests. Ancient Olympic athletes and spectators were male and the competitors performed naked. The black African ancestors of today's black Americans came by their running prowess out of a necessity to capture wild game for food. It was considered a great tribal honor to be chosen in these hunting parties in which only the swiftest and strongest could belong.

Travel journals and Frederick Douglass' autobiography mention foot races as forms of leisure activities among slaves before the Civil War. After this conflict, running competitions became highly organized and black participation was evident from the beginning. The walking races, the "Go As You Please" six-day races, and the Bunion Derbies all had black participation.

William Tecumseh Sherman Jackson was the first collegiate star as a middle distance runner. George Poage followed as the first black Olympian in 1904. He was followed by Dr. John B. Taylor and, in 1911, Howard Porter Drew, who was the first black world record holder of a sprint title.

Following World War I, black runners developed a reputation as sprinters and jumpers only, when in fact, the major shortcoming was a lack of quality instruction in the middle and long distance races at black colleges. In the 1920s, the so-called Golden Decade of Sports, the numbers of blacks on track teams at predominantly white schools could be counted on two hands.

All sorts of racist and supposedly objective and scientific theories were advanced to explain the "natural" superiority of black sprinters and jumpers when no such racially-based talent existed. As late as 1975, *Track and Field News* the bible of the sport, headlined an article entitled "IS BLACK FASTEST?" *Track and Field News* polled a cross-section of college coaches and found that 35 percent believed that blacks were physically superior to whites.

James "Doc" Counsilman, Indiana University's world famous swimming coach, felt that, "The Black athlete excels because he has more white muscle fibers, which are adapted for speed and power, than red fibers, which are adapted for endurance."[50] To this claim Wilbur Ross, the black coach at Winston-Salem State, answers, "This whole supremacy myth is a white athlete's cop-out. He has been so brainwashed by the racist white society that he has a preference role to fulfill."[51]

Brooks Johnson, the black Head Coach for the 1984 Olympic Men's team, says, "I call it the 'sprinter's syndrome' . . . the overpowering drive and compulsion to do what you have to do right now, to get the rewards right now."[52] Stan Wright believes part of the blame rests with black coaches themselves, noting, "We black coaches believed we were superior in the sprints and this was the only place we could run—or coach. This was a learned concept."[53]

Theories aside, no one can question the results. Deprived of equal opportunities for competition before 1960, black athletes have made up for lost time since then. In any historic record of this and most other sports,

the black American athlete is sure to be listed among the best of all time.

Notes

1. Delores T. Broots, "Black Olympians: 1948–1980" *Dollars and Sense*, June-July, 1983, 29.
2. Benjamin G. Raer, *American Sports* (Englewood Cliffs, N.J., 1983), 304.
3. Milton Campbell, telephone interview with author, 23 September 1985.
4. *Los Angeles Times*, Part VIII, 25 July 1984, 8.
5. Ibid., 9.
6. *Ebony*, November 1953.
7. Harold Braguieve, Interview with Kip Branch, 23 September 1985.
8. Nell Jackson, telephone interview with author, 4 December 1984.
9. *New York Times*, 18 March 1985, C-1.
10. *Los Angeles Times*, 24 July 1984.
11. *Los Angeles Times*, 24 July 1984.
12. Wilma Rudolph, *Wilma* (New York: New American Library, 1977), 79.
13. Nell Jackson, telephone interview with author, 4 December 1984.
14. *Ebony*, 1963.
15. *Los Angeles Times*, Part VIII, 25 July 1984, 16.
16. *Los Angeles Times*, Part VIII, (Mal Florence), 25 July 1984, 23.
17. Vince Matthews, *My Race Be Won* (New York: Charterhouse, 1974), 89.
18. *Newsweek*, 15 July 1968, 56.
19. Ibid.
20. James Michener, *Sports In America* (New York: Fawcett Crest, 1976), 208.
21. Dick Schaap, *The Perfect Jump* (New York: New American Library, 1976), 30.
22. Matthews, *My Race Be Won*, 9.
23. Schaap, *The Perfect Jump*, 30.
24. Harry Edwards, *The Sociology of Sport* (Homewood, IL.: The Dorsey Press, 1973), 72.
25. Harry Edwards, *Revolt of the Black Athlete* (New York: The Free Press, 1970), 55.
26. Ibid., 53.
27. *Ebony*, March 1968, 112.

28. *Ebony* March 1968, 188.
29. Ibid., 116.
30. Edwards, *Revolt Of The Black Athlete*, 131.
31. Ibid., 116.
32. *Sports Illustrated*, 28 February 1968, 25.
33. *Newsweek*, 15 July 1968, 57D.
34. Matthews, *My Race Be Won*, 173.
35. Edwards, *Revolt Of The Black Athlete*, 104.
36. *Newsweek*, 15 July 1984, 59.
37. Delores T. Broots, *Dollars and Sense*, 44.
38. Matthews, *My Race Be Won*, 198.
39. Schaap, *The Perfect Jump*, 94.
40. Ibid.
41. Ibid., 96.
42. *Ebony*, October 1971, 146.
43. Matthews, *My Race Be Won*, 191.
44. Ibid., 194.
45. Matthews, *My Race Be Won*, 355.
46. *Ebony*, September 1959, 110.
47. *Ebony*, May 1984, 100.
48. Nell Jackson, telephone interview with author, 4 December 1984.
49. Ibid.
50. *Track and Field News*, February 1975.
51. Ibid.
52. Ibid.
53. Ibid.

REFERENCE
SECTION

AFRICAN-AMERICAN OLYMPIC MEDALISTS, 1904 and 1908

1904	George C. Poage	Bronze	400-meter hurdles	No time available	Olympics at St. Louis, Mo.
1908	John Baxter Taylor	Gold	4–by–400-meter relay[1]	3:29.4 min.	Olympics at London, England

[1]White teamates: William Hamilton, Nathaniel Cartmel, Melvin Sheppard

Non-medalist

1908	W. C. Holmes	Event—Standing Broad Jump	Olympics at London, England

AFRICAN-AMERICAN AAU NATIONAL CHAMPIONS, THROUGH 1919

100 Meter Dash	Time	Affiliation
1912 Howard Porter Drew	10.0 s.	Springfield H.S. (Mass.)
1913 Howard Porter Drew	10.4 s.	Springfield H.S. (Mass.)

200 Meter Dash		
1913 Howard Porter Drew	22.8 s.	Springfield H.S. (Mass.)
1914 I.T. Howe	22.2 s.	Unattached, Boston
1915 Roy Morse	21.2 s.	Salem Crescent A.C., N.Y.

400 Meter Run		
1907 John Baxter Taylor	51.0 s.	University of Pennsylvania

AFRICAN-AMERICAN STARS ON WHITE COLLEGE TEAMS, THROUGH 1919

Wm. T.S. Jackson	1890-92	Amherst
Napoleon Marshall	1895-97	Harvard
Spencer Dickerson	1896-97	U. of Chicago
G.C.H. Burleigh	1896-98	U. of Illinois
George Poage	1903	Wisconsin
John Baxter Taylor	1903–1908	Pennsylvania
Howard Smith	1907	Pennsylvania
Dewey Rogers	1907	Pennsylvania
Ted Cable	1909-13	Harvard
Alexander Louis Jackson	1913	Harvard
Binga Dismond	1913	U. of Chicago
Cecil Lewis	1915	U. of Chicago
Irving Howe	1915	Dartmouth
W. Randolph Granger	1916	Dartmouth
J. Ferguson	1916	Dartmouth
Sol Butler	1915-18	Dubuque (Iowa)
Paul Robeson	1915-18	Rutgers
Howard Martin	1917	U. of Cincinnati
Jim Ravenelle	1917	New York University
Fred "Duke" Slater	1918-21	U. of Iowa
Ben Johnson	1918	Springfield (Mass.)
Howard Porter Drew	1918	Drake U. Law and Univ. of Southern California

AFRICAN-AMERICAN WORLD RECORD HOLDERS, THROUGH 1919

400-Meter Dash	**Time**	**Date**	**Site**
Ted Meredith	47.4 s.	May 27, 1916	Cambridge, Mass
Binga Dismond	47.4 s.	June 3, 1916	Evanston, Illinois
800-Meter Dash			
Ted Meredith	1:51.9 m.	July 8, 1912	Stockholm, Sweden
1,600-Meter Relay[1]			
Ted Meredith	3:16.6 m.	June 21, 1912	Stockholm, Sweden

[1]White Teammates—M. Sheppard, E. Lindberg, C. Reidpath

WOMAN'S AFRICAN-AMERICAN
AAU WINNERS THROUGH 1945

100 Meters

1938 Lula Hymes	Tuskegee	12.4
1940 Jean Lane	Wilberforce	12.0
1941 Jean Lane	Wilberforce	12.4
1942 Alice Coachman	Tuskegee	12.1
1945 Alice Coachman	Tuskegee	12.0

200 Meters

1928 Florence Wright	(Headlight AC)	27.4 (200 yards)
1937 Gertrude Johnson	(Mercury AC)	26.0
1941 Jean Lane	Wilberforce	25.2

100 Meters Hurdles

1937 Cora Gaines	Tuskegee	12.8
1941 Lelia Perry	Tuskegee	13.2
1942 Lillie Purifoy	Tuskegee	12.6
1944 Lillie Purifoy	Tuskegee	12.8
1945 Lillie Purifoy	Tuskegee	12.5

High Jump

1939 Alice Coachman	Tuskegee	5'-2"
1940 Alice Coachman	Tuskegee	4'-11"
1941 Alice Coachman	Tuskegee	5'-2 3/4"
1942 Alice Coachman	Tuskegee	4'-8"
1943 Alice Coachman	Tuskegee	5'-0"
1944 Alice Coachman	Tuskegee	5'-1 5/8"
1945 Alice Coachman	Tuskegee	5'-0"

Long Jump

1935 Etta Tate	(Unattached)	16'-6"
1936 Mable Smith	Tuskegee	18'-0"
1937 Lula Hymes	Tuskegee	17'-8 1/2"
1938 Lula Hymes	Tuskegee	17'-2"

Shot Put

1942 Ramona Harris	(Unattached)	37'-10 1/2"

Discus Throw

1944 Hattie Turner	Tuskegee	101'-7 3/4"

AMERICAN RECORDS HELD BY AFRICAN-AMERICANS AT THE END OF 1945
(MEN'S RECORDS)

60 yards

Ralph Metcalfe	6.1	March 11, 1933
Jesse Owens		March 9, 1935
Herbert Thompson		February 4, 1939
Bill Carter		March 15, 1941
Barney Ewell		February 7, 1942
Herbert Thompson		March 14, 1942
Herbert Thompson		March 27, 1943
Edward Conwell		February 26, 1944
Edward Conwell		March 9, 1946

100 yards

Jesse Owens	9.4	May 25, 1935

220 yards

Jesse Owens	20.3	May 25, 1935

880 yards

John Woodruff	1:47.7	March 14, 1940

1,000 yards

John Borican	2:08.8	March 11, 1939

Metric Distances

60 Meters

Jesse Owens	6.6	February 23, 1935
Herbert Thompson	6.6	February 25, 1939

100 Meters

Jesse Owens	10.2	June 20, 1936

400 Meters

James Herbert	48.4	March 14, 1940

800 Meters

John Woodruff	1:48.6	June 7, 1940

1600 Meter Relay

Stanford Braun, Harold Bogrow, James McPoland, JAMES HERBERT*	3:15.0	March 14, 1940

4 Mile Relay

M. Truitt, JAMES SMITH,* T. Deckard, D. Lash	17:16.1	April 23, 1937

220 Yard Hurdles

Harrison Dillard	22.5	June 8, 1946

Running High Jump

Ed Burke	6'9 1/4"	February 27, 1937
Mel Walker	6'9 3/4"	March 20, 1937

Running Broad Jump

Jesse Owens	26'8 1/4"	May 25, 1935

Women's Records

50 yard run

Elizabeth Robinson	5.8	July 27, 1929

50 Meter Run

Alice Coachman	6.4	July 14, 1944

100 yard dash

Jean Lane	10.9	May 29, 1940

220 yard run

Elizabeth Robinson	25.1	June 20, 1931

Running Broad Jump

Lula Mae Hymes	18'1 1/2"	September 3, 1939

400 Meter Relay

Tuskegee Institute (Lucy Newell, Jessie Abbott, Rowena Harris, Lula Mae Hymes)	49.3	July 13, 1940

*In relays, names in capitals are black runners; other relay runners are white.

WORLD RECORDS HELD BY AFRICAN-AMERICANS AT THE END OF 1945

100 Meters

Jesse Owens	10.2	June 20, 1936

200 Meters

Jesse Owens	20.7	August 5, 1936

4 × 100 Meter Relay

Jesse Owens Ralph Metcalfe Frank Draper (white) Frank Wykoff (white)	39.8	August 9, 1936

Long Jump

Jesse Owens	8.13 m (26' 81/4")	May 25, 1935

MEN'S AFRICAN-AMERICAN NCAA WINNERS THROUGH 1945

100 Meters

1925	William DeHart Hubbard	(Michigan)	9.8	100 yards
1932	Ralph Metcalfe	(Marquette)	10.2	
1933	Ralph Metcalfe	(Marquette)	9.4	100 yards
1934	Ralph Metcalfe	(Marquette)	9.7	100 yards
1935	Jesse Owens	(Ohio State)	9.8	100 yards
1936	Jesse Owens	(Ohio State)	10.2	
1938	Mozelle Ellerbe	(Tuskegee)	9.7	100 yards
1939	Mozelle Ellerbe	(Tuskegee)	9.8	100 yards
1940	Barney Ewell	(Penn State)	9.6	100 yards
1941	Barney Ewell	(Penn State)	9.6	100 yards
1944	Buddy Young	(Illinois)	9.7	100 yards

200 Meters

1931	Eddie Tolan	(Michigan)	21.5	200 yards
1932	Ralph Metcalfe	(Marquette)	20.3	
1933	Ralph Metcalfe	(Marquette)	20.4	200 yards
1934	Ralph Metcalfe	(Marquette)	20.9	200 yards
1935	Jesse Owens	(Ohio State)	21.5	200 yards
1936	Jesse Owens	(Ohio State)	21.3	
1937	Ben Johnson	(Columbia)	21.3	200 yards
1938	Mark Robinson	(Oregon)	21.3	200 yards
1940	Barney Ewell	(Penn State)	21.1	200 yards
1941	Barney Ewell	(Penn State)	21.1	200 yards
1944	Buddy Young	(Illinois)	21.6	200 yards

400 Meters

1935	James Luvalle	(UCLA)	47.7	440 yards
1936	Archie Williams	(California)	47.0	440 yards
1944	Elmore Harris	(Morgan State)	47.9	440 yards

800 Meters

1937	John Woodruff	(Pittsburgh)	1:50.3	880 yards
1938	John Woodruff	(Pittsburgh)	1:52.3	880 yards
1939	John Woodruff	(Pittsburgh)	1:51.3	880 yards

110 Meter High Hurdles

1940	Ed Dugger	(Tufts)	13.9	120 yards

High Jump

1936	Mel Walker	(Ohio State)	6'-6 ⅛"
	Dave Albritton	(Ohio State)	
1937	Gil Cruter	(Colorado)	6'-6 ¼"
	Dave Albritton	(Ohio State)	
1938	Gil Cruter	(Colorado)	6'-8 ¾"
	Dave Albritton	(Ohio State)	
1942	Adam Berry	(Southern U.)	6'-7 ¾"

Long Jump

1923	DeHart Hubbard	(Michigan)	25' 2"
1925	DeHart Hubbard	(Michigan)	25' 10⅞"
1929	Ed Gordon	(Iowa)	24' 8½"
1930	Ed Gordon	(Iowa)	25' 0"
1931	Ed Gordon	(Iowa)	24' 11⅜"
1933	John Brooks	(Chicago)	24' 4¾"
1935	Jesse Owens	(Ohio State)	26' 1⅜"
1936	Jesse Owens	(Ohio State)	25' 10⅞"
1937	Kermit King	(Pittsburgh)	25' 3¼"
1938	William Lacefield	(UCLA)	25' 1⅛"
1940	Jackie Robinson	(UCLA)	24' 10¼"

Discus Throw

1940	Archie Harris	(Indiana)	162'-4¼"
1941	Archie Harris	(Indiana)	174'-8¾"

Javelin Throw

1932	George Williams	Hampton	215'-0"

AFRICAN-AMERICAN OLYMPIANS

Year	Name	Medal	Event	Result	City
1924	William DeHart Hubbard	Gold	Long Jump	24'5"	Paris
1924	Edward Gourdin	Silver	Long Jump	23'10"	Paris
1924	Earl Johnson	Bronze	10,000 Meters	—	Paris
1932	Eddie Tolan	Gold	100 Meters	10.3	Los Angeles
1932	Eddie Tolan	Gold	200 Meters	21.2	Los Angeles
1932	Ralph Metcalfe	Silver	100 Meters	10.3	Los Angeles
1932	Ralph Metcalfe	Bronze	200 Meters	21.5	Los Angeles
1932	Edward Gordon	Gold	Long Jump	25'0 ¾"	Los Angeles
1936	Cornelius Johnson	Gold	High Jump	6'8"	Berlin
1936	David Albritton	Silver	High Jump	6'6 ¾"	Berlin
1936	Jesse Owens	Gold	100 Meters	10.3	Berlin
1936	Jesse Owens	Gold	200 Meters	20.7	Berlin
1936	Jesse Owens	Gold	Long Jump	25'5 ½"	Berlin
1936	Jesse Owens**	Gold	400M- Relay	39.8	Berlin
1936	Archie Williams	Gold	400 Meters	46.5	Berlin
1936	James Luvalle	Bronze	400 Meters	46.8	Berlin
1936	John Woodruff	Gold	800 Meters	1:52.9	Berlin
1936	Mack Robinson	Silver	200 Meters	21.1	Berlin
1936	Ralph Metcalfe**	Gold	400M- Relay	39.8	Berlin
1936	Ralph Metcalfe	Silver	100 Meters	10.4	Berlin
1936	Fritz Pollard, Jr.	Bronze	110M- Hurdles	14.4	Berlin

**White teammates on Gold Medal 400 Meter Relay team were Frank Wykoff, Foy Draper.

MEN'S AFRICAN-AMERICAN AAU WINNERS
THROUGH 1945

100 Meters

1912 Howard Drew	(Springfield HS)	10.0	100 yards
1913 Howard Drew	(Springfield HS)	10.0	100 yards
1916 Andy Ward	(Chicago AA)	10.0	100 yards
1917 Andy Ward	(Chicago AA)	10.2	100 yards
1929 Eddie Tolan	(Michigan)	10.0	100 yards
1930 Eddie Tolan	(Michigan)	9.7	100 yards
1932 Ralph Metcalfe	(Marquette)	10.6	
1933 Ralph Metcalfe	(Marquette)	10.5	
1934 Ralph Metcalfe	(Marquette)	10.4	
1935 Eulace Peacock	(Shore AC)	10.2	
1936 Jesse Owens	(Ohio State)	10.4	
1938 Ben Johnson	(NY Curb Exchange)	10.7	
1941 Barney Ewell	(US Army)	10.3	
1944 Buddy Young	(Illinois)	10.5	
1945 Barney Ewell	(US Army)	10.3	

200 Meters

1913 Howard Drew	(Springfield HS)	22.8	220 yards
1916 Andy Ward	(Chicago AA)	21.6	220 yards
1917 Andy Ward	(Chicago AA)	22.2	220 yards
1929 Eddie Tolan	(Michigan)	21.9	220 yards
1931 Eddie Tolan	(Unattached)	21.0	220 yards
1932 Ralph Metcalfe	(Marquette)	21.5	
1933 Ralph Metcalfe	(Marquette)	21.1	
1934 Ralph Metcalfe	(Marquette)	21.3	
1935 Ralph Metcalfe	(Marquette U. Club)	21.0	
1936 Ralph Metcalfe	(Marquette U. Club)	21.2	
1938 Mack Robinson	(Oregon)	21.3	
1939 Barney Ewell	(Penn State)	21.0	
1945 Elmore Harris	(Shore AC)	21.9	

400 Meters

1914 Ted Meredith	(Meadow Club)	50.2	440 yards
1915 Ted Meredith	(Meadow Club)	47.0	440 yards
1925 Cecil Cooke	(Salem Crescent AC)	49.2	440 yards
1944 Elmore Harris	(Shore AC)	48.0	

800 Meters

1934 Ben Eastman	(SF Olympic Club)	1:50.4
1937 John Woodruff	(Pittsburgh)	1:50.0
1942 John Borican	(Asbury Park AC)	1:51.2
1944 Robert Kelly	(Illinois)	1:51.8
1945 Robert Kelly	(Illinois)	1:54.1

10,000 Meters

1921	Earl Johnson	(Thomson Steel)	25:53.4
1922	Earl Johnson	(Thomson Steel)	25:33.0
1923	Earl Johnson	(Thomson Steel)	26:52.0

110 Meter Hurdles

1918	Earl Thomson	(Canada)	15.2	110 yards
1921	Earl Thomson	(Boston AA/Can.)	15.0	110 yards
1922	Earl Thomson	(Unattached/Can.)	15.3	110 yards

High Jump

1932	Cornelius Johnson	(Calif. HS)	6'6 ⅝"
1933	Cornelius Johnson	(Calif. HS)	6'7"
1934	Cornelius Johnson	(Compton JC)	6'8 ⅝"
1935	Cornelius Johnson	(Compton JC)	6'7"
1936	Cornelius Johnson	(Compton JC)	6'8"
	Mel Walker	(Ohio State)	6'8"
	Dave Albritton	(Ohio State)	6'8"
1937	Dave Albritton	(Ohio State)	6'8 ⅝"
1938	Dave Albritton	(Ohio State)	6'7"
	Mel Walker	(Unattached)	6'7"
1942	Adam Berry	(Southern U)	6'7"
1945	Dave Albritton	(Unattached)	6'5 ¾"
	Josh Williamson	(US Army)	6'5 ¾"

Long Jump

1920	Sol Butler	(Dubuque Col.)	24'-8"
1921	Ned Gourdin	(Harvard)	23'-7 ¾"
1922	William DeHart Hubbard	(Unattached)	24'-5 ⅛"
1923	William DeHart Hubbard	(Michigan)	24'-7 ¾"
1924	William DeHart Hubbard	(Michigan)	24'-0"
1925	William DeHart Hubbard	(Unattached)	25'-4 ⅜"
1926	William DeHart Hubbard	(Century AC)	25'-2 ½"
1927	William DeHart Hubbard	(Unattached)	25'-8 ¾"
1929	Ed Gordon, Jr.	(U. of Iowa)	24'-4 ¼"
1933	Jesse Owens	(Ohio H.S.)	24'-6 ⅜"
1934	Jesse Owens	(Ohio State)	25'-0 ⅞"
1935	Eulace Peacock	(Shore AC)	26'-3"
1936	Jesse Owens	(Ohio State)	26'-3"
1937	Kermit King	(Pittsburgh)	25'-1 ½"
1938	William Lacefield	(UCLA)	25'-0 3/10"
1939	William Lacefield	(Unattached)	25'-5 ½"
1945	Herb Douglas	(Unattached)	24'-0 ⅛"

Triple Jump

1922	William DeHart Hubbard	(Unattached)	48'-1 ½"
1923	William DeHart Hubbard	(Michigan)	47'-0 ½"
1944	Don Barksdale	(US Army)	47'-2 ⅞"

Shot Put

1939 Lilburn Williams	(Xavier)	53'-7"

Discus Throw

1941 Archie Harris	(Unattached)	167'-9 ½"

Decathlon

1940 William Watson	(Unattached)	7523 points
1941 John Borican	(Asbury Park AC)	5666
1943 William Watson	(Detroit Police)	5994

BLACK COLLEGE CONFERENCE WINNERS

	CIAA	SWAC	SIAC	EIAC	SCAC	MWAC
1924	Hampton					
1925	Hampton					
1926	Hampton					
1927	Hampton					
1928	Lincoln					
1929	Hampton					
1930	Morgan					
1931	Hampton					
1932	St. Paul					
1933	Morgan					Wilberforce
1934	Va. Union					Wilberforce
1935	Hampton					Wilberforce
1936	Va. State & Morgan					Wilberforce
1937	Hampton					No Meet
1938	Va. State	Bishop	Xavier			Wilberforce
1939	Va. State	Bishop	Xavier			Lincoln U. (Mo.)
1940		Prairie View			Alcorn A & M	Lincoln U. (Mo.)
1941	Hampton	Southern			Dillard	
1942		Southern			Alcorn A & M	
1943		Southern				
1944		Prairie View			Tougaloo	
1945	Morgan	Wiley			Okolona	

BLACK COLLEGE CONFERENCE CHAMPIONS

CIAA			SWAC	
1950	Morgan St.	Ed Hurt	Prairie View	Jimmy Stephens
1951	Morgan St.	Ed Hurt	Prairie View	Jimmy Stephens
1952	Morgan St.	Ed Hurt	Prairie View	Jimmy Stephens
1953	Morgan St.	Ed Hurt	Prairie View	Hugh McKinnis
1954	Morgan St.	Ed Hurt	Southern U.	Robert Smith
1955	Morgan St.	Ed Hurt	Texas Southern	Stan Wright
1956	Morgan St.	Ed Hurt	Prairie View	Hugh McKinnis
1957	Morgan St.	Ed Hurt	Texas Southern	Stan Wright
1958	Morgan St.	Ed Hurt	Prairie View	Leroy Moore
1959	Winston-Salem	Wilbur Ross	Southern U.	Eugene Thomas
1960	Winston-Salem	Wilbur Ross	Southern U.	Eugene Thomas
1961	Maryland E-S	Wilbur Ross	Texas Southern	Stan Wright
1962	Maryland E-S	Wilbur Ross	Texas Southern	Stan Wright
1963	Maryland E-S	Wilbur Ross	Texas Southern	Stan Wright
1964	N.C Central	Leroy Walker	Southern U.	Robert Smith
1965	N.C. Central	Leroy Walker	Southern U.	Robert Smith
1966	(No Title)		Southern U.	Dick Hill
1967	Maryland E-S	Cap Anderson	Texas Southern	Stan Wright
1968	Maryland E-S	Cap Anderson	Southern U.	Dick Hill
1969	J.C. Smith	Ken Powell	Prairie View	Hoover Wright
1970	J.C. Smith	Ken Powell	Prairie View	Hoover Wright
1971	N.C. Central	Leroy Walker	Southern U.	Dick Hill
1972	Norfolk St.	Dick Price	Texas Southern	Dave Bethany
1973	Norfolk St.	Dick Price	Texas Southern	Dave Bethany
1974	Norfolk St.	Dick Price	Texas Southern	Dave Bethany
1975	Norfolk St.	Dick Price	Jackson St.	Martin Epps
1976	Norfolk St.	Dick Price	Jackson St.	Martin Epps
1977	Virginia St.	George Williams	Jackson St.	Martin Epps
1978	St. Augustine	George Williams	Jackson St.	Martin Epps
1979	St. Augustine	George Williams	Texas Southern	Dave Bethany
1980	St. Augustine	George Williams	Texas Southern	Dave Bethany
1981	Virginia St.	William Bennett	Texas Southern	Dave Bethany
1982	St. Augustine	George Williams	Texas Southern	Dave Bethany
1983	St. Augustine	George Williams	Jackson St.	Martin Epps
1984	St. Augustine	George Williams	Texas Southern	Dave Bethany

SIAC			MEAC	
1951	Xavier (La.)	Al Priestley		
1952	Florida A&M	Robert Griffin		
1953	Xavier (La.)	Al Priestley		
1954	Xavier (La.)	Al Priestley		
1955	Florida A&M	Robert Griffin		
1956	Florida A&M	Robert Griffin		
1957	Xavier (La.)	Al Priestley		
1958	Xavier (La.)	Al Priestley		
1959	Florida A&M	Robert Griffin		
1960	Florida A&M	Robert Griffin		
1961	Florida A&M	Robert Griffin		
1962	Florida A&M	Dick Hill		
1963	Florida A&M	Dick Hill		
1964	Florida A&M	Dick Hill		
1965	Morehouse	Darlington		
1966	Florida A&M	Bobby Lang		
1967	Florida A&M	Bobby Lang		
1968	Florida A&M	Bobby Lang		
1969	Florida A&M	Bobby Lang		
1970	Florida A&M	Bobby Lang		
1971	Florida A&M	Bobby Lang		
1972	Florida A&M	Bobby Lang	N.C. Central	Leroy Walker
1973	Albany State	Robert Cross	N.C. Central	Leroy Walker
1974	Albany State	Robert Cross	N.C. Central	Leroy Walker
1975	Albany State	Robert Cross	(No Title)	
1976	Florida A&M	Bobby Lang	Delaware St.	Joe Burden
1977	Florida A&M	Bobby Lang	S.C. State	Robert Johnson
1978	Albany State	Robert Cross	S.C. State	Robert Johnson
1979	Florida A&M	Bobby Lang	S.C. State	Robert Johnson
1980	Albany State	Robert Cross	Florida A&M	Bobby Lang
1981	Albany State	Robert Cross	S.C. State	Robert Johnson
1982	Albany State	Robert Cross	Florida A&M	Bobby Lang
1983	Albany State	Robert Cross	S.C. State	Robert Johnson
1984	Albany State	Robert Cross	S.C. State	Robert Johnson

BLACK COLLEGE WOMEN'S CONFERENCE CHAMPIONS

SIAC			MEAC	
1980	Alabama A&M	Joe Henderson	Howard	William Moultrie
1981	Alabama A&M	Joe Henderson	Delaware St.	Joe Burden
1982	Alabama A&M	Joe Henderson	S.C. State	Robert Johnson
1983	Alabama A&M	Joe Henderson	S.C. State	Robert Johnson
1984	Alabama A&M	Joe Henderson	S.C. State	Robert Johnson

CIAA			SWAC	
1974			Prairie View	Barbara Jacket
1975			Prairie View	Barbara Jacket
1976			Prairie View	Barbara Jacket
1977	Virginia St.	William Bennett	Prairie View	Barbara Jacket
1978	St. Augustine	George Williams	Prairie View	Barbara Jacket
1979	St. Augustine	George Williams	Prairie View	Barbara Jacket
1980	St. Augustine	George Williams	Prairie View	Barbara Jacket
1981	St. Augustine	George Williams	Texas Southern	Dave Bethany
1982	St. Augustine	George Williams	Prairie View	Barbara Jacket
1983	St. Augustine	George Williams	Jackson St.	Martin Epps
1984	St. Augustine	George Williams	Prairie View	Barbara Jacket

EVOLUTION OF WORLD RECORDS
(African-Americans in Capitals)
100-meter dash

	Runner	Time	Date
1.	HOWARD PORTER DREW	10.4 seconds	JUNE 8, 1912
2.	Charley Paddock	10.4 seconds	APRIL 23, 1921
3.	EDDIE TOLAN	10.4 seconds	AUGUST 8, 1929
4.	Percy Williams (Canada)	10.3 seconds	AUGUST 9, 1930
5.	EDDIE TOLAN	10.3 seconds	AUGUST 1, 1932
6.	RALPH METCALFE	10.3 seconds	AUGUST 12, 1933
7.	EULACE PEACOCK	10.2 seconds	AUGUST 6, 1934
8.	Christian Berger (Neth.)	10.3 seconds	AUGUST 26, 1934
9.	RALPH METCALFE	10.3 seconds	SEPTEMBER 15, 1934
10.	RALPH METCALFE	10.3 seconds	SEPTEMBER 23, 1934
11.	Takayoshi Yoshioka (Jap.)	10.3 seconds	JUNE 15, 1935
12.	JESSE OWENS	10.2 seconds	JUNE 20, 1936
13.	Harold Davis	10.2 seconds	JUNE 6, 1941
14.	Lloyd LaBeach (Panama)	10.2 seconds	MAY 15, 1948
15.	NORWOOD "BARNEY" EWELL	10.2 seconds	JULY 9, 1948
16.	Emm M. Bailey (England)	10.2 seconds	AUGUST 25, 1951
17.	Heinz Futtere (Germany)	10.2 seconds	OCTOBER 31, 1954
18.	Bobby Morrow	10.2 seconds	MAY 19, 1956
19.	Bobby Morrow	10.2 seconds	MAY 26, 1956
20.	IRA MURCHISON	10.2 seconds	JUNE 1, 1956
21.	Bobby Morrow	10.2 seconds	JUNE 22 1956
22.	IRA MURCHISON	10.2 seconds	JUNE 29, 1956

	Runner	Time	Date
23.	Bobby Morrow	10.2 seconds	JUNE 29, 1956
24.	WILLIE WILLIAMS	10.1 seconds	AUGUST 3, 1956
25.	IRA MURCHISON	10.1 seconds	AUGUST 4, 1956
26.	LEAMON KING	10.1 seconds	OCTOBER 27, 1956
27.	RAY NORTON	10.1 seconds	APRIL 18, 1959
28.	Harry Jerome (Canada)	10.0 seconds	JUNE 21, 1960
29.	Armin Hary (Germany)	10.0 seconds	JULY 15, 1960
30.	Horacio Esteves (Ven.)	10.0 seconds	AUGUST 15, 1964
31.	BOB HAYES	10.0 seconds	OCTOBER 15, 1964
32.	JIM HINES	10.0 seconds	MAY 27, 1967
33.	Paul Nash (South Africa)	10.0 seconds	APRIL 2, 1968
34.	OLIVER FORD	10.0 seconds	MAY 31, 1967
35.	CHARLIE GREENE	10.0 seconds	JUNE 10, 1968
36.	Roger Bambuck	10.0 seconds	JUNE 20, 1968
37.	JIM HINES	9.9 seconds	JUNE 10, 1968
38.	RONNIE RAY SMITH	9.9 seconds	JUNE 20, 1968
39.	CHARLIE GREENE	9.9 seconds	JUNE 20, 1968
40.	JIM HINES	9.9 seconds	OCTOBER 14, 1968
41.	EDDIE HART	9.9 seconds	JULY 1, 1972
42.	REY ROBINSON	9.9 seconds	JULY 1, 1972
43.	STEVE WILLIAMS	9.9 seconds	JUNE 21, 1974
44.	Silvio Leonard (Cuba)	9.9 seconds	JUNE 5, 1975
45.	STEVE WILLIAMS	9.9 seconds	JULY 16, 1975
46.	STEVE WILLIAMS	9.9 seconds	AUGUST 22, 1975
47.	STEVE WILLIAMS	9.9 seconds	MARCH 27, 1976
48.	HARVEY GLANCE	9.9 seconds	APRIL 3, 1976
49.	HARVEY GLANCE	9.9 seconds	MAY 1, 1976
50.	Don Quarrie (Jamaica)	9.9 seconds	MAY 22, 1976
51.	CARL LEWIS	9.86 seconds	AUGUST 25, 1991

200-meter dash

		Time	Date
1.	EDDIE TOLAN	21.1 seconds	AUGUST 9, 1929
2.	RALPH METCALFE	21.1 seconds	JULY 28, 1933
3.	JESSE OWENS	21.1 seconds	AUGUST 4, 1936
4.	JESSE OWENS	20.7 seconds	AUGUST 5, 1936
5.	Mel Patton	20.7 seconds	JULY 10, 1948
6.	ANDY STANFIELD	20.6 seconds	MAY 26, 1951
7.	ANDY STANFIELD	20.6 seconds	JUNE 28, 1952
8.	Than Baker	20.6 seconds	JUNE 23, 1956
9.	ANDY STANFIELD	20.6 seconds	JUNE 23, 1956
10.	Bobby Morrow	20.6 seconds	NOVEMBER 27, 1957
11.	Manfred Germar (Ger.)	20.6 seconds	OCTOBER 1, 1958
12.	RAY NORTON	20.6 seconds	MARCH 19, 1960

	Runner	Time	Date
13.	RAY NORTON	20.6 seconds	APRIL 30, 1960
14.	STONE JOHNSON	20.5 seconds	JULY 2, 1960
15.	RAY NORTON	20.5 seconds	JULY 2, 1960
16.	Livio Berruti (Italy)	20.5 seconds	SEPTEMBER 3, 1960
17.	PAUL DRAYTON	20.5 seconds	JUNE 23, 1962
18.	HENRY CARR	20.3 seconds	MARCH 23, 1963
19.	HENRY CARR	20.2 seconds	APRIL 4, 1964
20.	TOMMIE SMITH	20.0 seconds	JUNE 11, 1966
21.	TOMMIE SMITH	19.8 seconds	OCTOBER 16, 1968
22.	Don Quarrie (Jamaica)	19.8 seconds	JUNE 21, 1975
23.	JAMES MALLARD	19.8 seconds	MAY 13, 1979
24.	Pietro Mennea (Italy)	19.8 seconds	SEPTEMBER 3, 1979
25.	JAMES SANFORD	19.7 seconds	APRIL 19, 1980

400-meter dash

1.	TED MEREDITH	47.4 seconds	MAY 27, 1916
2.	BINGA DISMOND	47.4 seconds	JUNE 3, 1916
3.	Emerson Spencer	47.0 seconds	MAY 12, 1928
4.	Ben Eastman	46.4 seconds	MARCH 26, 1932
5.	Bill Carr	46.2 seconds	AUGUST 5, 1932
6.	ARCHIE WILLIAMS	46.1 seconds	JUNE 19, 1936
7.	Rudolf Harbig (Germany)	46.0 seconds	AUGUST 12, 1939
8.	Herb McKinley (Jamaica)	45.9 seconds	JULY 2, 1948
9.	George Rhoden (Jamaica)	45.8 seconds	AUGUST 22, 1950
10.	LOU JONES	45.4 seconds	MARCH 18, 1955
11.	LOU JONES	45.2 seconds	JUNE 30, 1956
12.	OTIS DAVIS	44.9 seconds	SEPTEMBER 6, 1960
13.	Mike Larrabee	44.9 seconds	SEPTEMBER 12, 1964
14.	TOMMIE SMITH	44.5 seconds	MAY 20, 1967
15.	LARRY JAMES	44.1 seconds	SEPTEMBER 14, 1968
16.	LEE EVANS	43.8 seconds	OCTOBER 18, 1968
17.	BUTCH REYNOLDS	43.29 seconds	AUGUST 17, 1988

400-meter hurdles

1.	Gert Potgieter (S. Afr.)	49.3 seconds	APRIL 16, 1960
2.	Sal Morale (Italy)	49.2 seconds	SEPTEMBER 14, 1962
3.	Warren Cawley	49.1 seconds	SEPTEMBER 13, 1964
4.	Geoff Vanderstock	48.1 seconds	SEPTEMBER 11, 1968
5.	John Akii-Bua (Uganda)	47.8 seconds	SEPTEMBER 2, 1972
6.	EDWIN MOSES	47.64 seconds	JULY 25, 1976
7.	EDWIN MOSES	47.45 seconds	JULY 11, 1977

	Runner	Time	Date
8.	EDWIN MOSES	47.13 seconds	JULY 3, 1980
9.	EDWIN MOSES	47.02 seconds	AUGUST 31, 1983
10.	KEVIN YOUNG	46.78 seconds	1992

110-meter hurdles

1.	HARRISON DILLARD	13.6 seconds	APRIL 17, 1948
2.	Dick Attlesley	13.5 seconds	MAY 13, 1950
3.	Jack Davis	13.4 seconds	JUNE 22, 1956
4.	LEE CALHOUN	13.2 seconds	AUGUST 21, 1960
5.	EARL McCULLOCH	13.2 seconds	JULY 16, 1967
6.	WILLIE DAVENPORT	13.2 seconds	JULY 4, 1969
7.	ROD MILBURN	13.0 seconds	JUNE 25, 1971
8.	RENALDO NEHEMIAH	12.93 seconds	AUGUST 19, 1981
9.	ROGER KINGDOM	12.92 seconds	AUGUST 16, 1989

long jump

1.	Peter O'Connell	7.61 meters	AUGUST 5, 1901
2.	EDWARD GOURDIN	7.69 meters	JULY 23, 1921
3.	WILLIAM DeHART HUBBARD	7.89 meters	JUNE 13, 1925
4.	Shuhei Nambu (Japan)	7.98 meters	OCTOBER 27, 1931
5.	JESSE OWENS	8.13 meters	MAY 25, 1935
6.	RALPH BOSTON	8.21 meters	AUGUST 12, 1960
7.	RALPH BOSTON	8.24 meters	MAY 27, 1961
8.	RALPH BOSTON	8.28 meters	JULY 16, 1961
9.	Igor T.-Ovanesyan (Rus.)	8.31 meters	JUNE 10, 1962
10.	RALPH BOSTON	8.31 meters	AUGUST 15, 1964
11.	RALPH BOSTON	8.34 meters	SEPTEMBER 12, 1964
12.	RALPH BOSTON	8.35 meters	MAY 29, 1965
13.	BOB BEAMON (29′ 2½″)	8.90 meters	OCTOBER 18, 1968
14.	MIKE POWELL	8.95 meters	AUGUST 30, 1991

high jump

1.	George Horine	2.00 meters	MAY 18, 1912
2.	CORNELIUS JOHNSON	2.07 meters	JULY 12, 1936
3.	DAVE ALBRITTON	2.07 meters	JULY 12, 1936
4.	MELVIN WALKER	2.09 meters	AUGUST 12, 1937
5.	Lester Steers	2.11 meters	JUNE 17, 1941
6.	WALTER DAVIS	2.12 meters	JUNE 27, 1953
7.	CHARLES DUMAS	2.15 meters	JUNE 29, 1956
8.	Yuri Styepanov (Russia)	2.16 meters	JULY 13, 1957
9.	JOHN THOMAS	2.17 meters	APRIL 30, 1960

	Runner	Time	Date
10.	JOHN THOMAS	2.18 meters	JUNE 24, 1960
11.	Valeri Brumel (Russia)	2.23 meters	JUNE 18, 1961
12.	Zhu Jianhua (China)	2.38 meters	SEPTEMBER 22, 1983

decathlon

1.	Bob Mathias	7,690 points	JULY 1-2, 1952
2.	RAFER JOHNSON	7,758 points	JUNE 10-11, 1955
3.	Vasiliy Kusnyetsov (Rus.)	7,760 points	MAY 17-18, 1958
4.	RAFER JOHNSON	7,896 points	JULY 27-28, 1958
5.	Vasiliy Kusnyetsov (Rus.)	7,957 points	MAY 16-17, 1959
6.	RAFER JOHNSON	8,063 points	JULY 8-9, 1960

4 X 100-meter relay

1.	I. Moller, C. Luther T. Persson, K. Lindberg	42.5 seconds	JULY 8, 1912
2.	(The record was improved 7 times between 1912 and 1935)		
3.	JESSE OWENS, RALPH METCALFE Frank Wykoff, Fred Draper	39.8 seconds	AUGUST 9, 1936
4.	IRA MURCHISON, LEAMON KING Bobby Morrow, T. Baker	39.5 seconds	DECEMBER 1, 1956
5.	HAYES JONES, Paul Drayton, C. FRAZIER, Frank Budd	39.1 seconds	JULY 15, 1961
6.	Paul Drayton, BOB HAYES G. Ashworth, R. STEBBINS	39.0 seconds	OCTOBER 21, 1964
7.	EARL McCULLOCH, O.J. SIMPSON, F. Kuller, L. Miller	38.6 seconds	JUNE 17, 1967
8.	CHARLIE GREEN, MEL PENDER RONNIE SMITH, JIM HINES	38.2 seconds	OCTOBER 20, 1968
9.	LARRY BLACK, ROBERT TAYLOR, GERALD TINKER, EDDIE HART	38.2 seconds	SEPTEMBER 10, 1972
10.	STEVE RIDDICK, STEVE WILLIAMS, B. COLLINS, CLIFF WILEY	38.03 seconds	SEPTEMBER 3, 1977
11.	EMMITT KING, WILLIE GAULT, CALVIN SMITH, CARL LEWIS	37.86 seconds	AUGUST 10, 1983
12.	RON BROWN, SAM GRADDY, CALVIN SMITH, CARL LEWIS	37.83 seconds	AUGUST, 1984
13.	Max Morindere, Daniel Sangouma, Jean Charles Trouabal, Banis Marie-Rose	37.79 seconds	SEPTEMBER 1, 1990
14.	ANDRE CASON, LEROY BURRELL, DENNIS MITCHELL, CARL LEWIS	37.50 seconds	SEPTEMBER 1, 1991
15.	LEROY BURRELL, DENNIS MITCHELL, MIKE MARSH, CARL LEWIS	37.40 seconds	AUGUST 8, 1992

4 X 400-meter relay

	Runner	Time	Date
1.	Irish-American A.C.	3:18.2 minutes	SEPTEMBER 4, 1911
2.	(The record was lowered 7 times between 1911 and 1959)		
3.	OTIS DAVIS, J. Yerman,		
	E. Young, G. Davis	3:02.2 minutes	SEPTEMBER 8, 1960
4.	HENRY CARR, ULIS WILLIAMS,		
	O. Cassell, M. Larrabee	3:00.7 minutes	OCTOBER 21, 1964
5.	LEE EVANS, TOMMIE SMITH,		
	THERIN LEWIS, R. Frey	2:59.6 minutes	JULY 24, 1966
6.	LEE EVANS, RON FREEMAN,		
	VINCE MATTHEWS, LARRY JAMES	2:56.1 minutes	OCTOBER 20, 1968
7.	STEVE LEWIS, DANNY EVERETT, Steve Robinzine,	2:56.16 minutes	OCTOBER 1, 1988
	HAROLD REYNOLDS		
8.	QUINCY WATTS, ANDREW YALMON,		
	MICHAEL JOHNSON, STEVE LEWIS	2:55.74 minutes	AUGUST 8, 1992

Women's 100-meter dash

1.	Stella Walsh (Poland)	11.7 seconds	AUGUST 26, 1934
2.	(The record was lowered 4 times between 1934 and 1959)		
3.	WILMA RUDOLPH	11.3 seconds	SEPTEMBER 2, 1960
4.	WILMA RUDOLPH	11.2 seconds	JULY 19, 1961
5.	WYOMIA TYUS	11.2 seconds	OCTOBER 15, 1964
6.	Irene Kirszentein (Pol.)	11.1 seconds	JULY 9, 1965
7.	WYOMIA TYUS	11.1 seconds	JULY 31, 1965
8.	BARBARA FERRELL	11.1 seconds	JULY 2, 1967
9.	WYOMIA TYUS	11.0 seconds	OCTOBER 15, 1968
10.	Renate Meissner (GDR)	10.9 seconds	AUGUST 20, 1972
11.	Renate Meissner (GDR)	10.8 seconds	JULY 20, 1973
12.	EVELYN ASHFORD	10.79 seconds	JUNE 3, 1983
13.	EVELYN ASHFORD	10.76 seconds	AUGUST 22, 1984
14.	FLORENCE GRIFFITH-JOYNER	10.49 seconds	JULY 16, 1988

Women's 200-meter dash

1.	Stella Walsh (Poland)	23.6 seconds	AUGUST 15, 1935
2.	(The record was lowered 2 times between 1935 and 1959)		
3.	WILMA RUDOLPH	22.9 seconds	JULY 9, 1960
4.	FLORENCE GRIFFITH-JOYNER	21.34 seconds	SEPTEMBER, 1988

Women's 4 X 100-meter relay

	Runner	Time	Date
1.	Albus, Krauss, Dollinger, Dorffeldt	46.6 seconds	AUGUST 8, 1936
2.	MAE FAGGS, BARBARA JONES, CATHERINE HARDY, Brenda Moreau	45.9 seconds	JULY 27, 1952
3.	(The record was lowered 5 times between 1952 and 1959)		
4.	MARTHA HUDSON, LUCINDA WILLIAMS, BARBARA JONES, WILMA RUDOLPH	44.4 seconds	SEPTEMBER 7, 1960
5.	WILLYE WHITE, WILMA RUDLOPH, ERNESTINE POLLARD, VIVIAN BROWN	44.3 seconds	JULY 15, 1961
6.	WILLYE WHITE, WYOMIA TYUS, MARILYN WHITE, EDITH McGUIRE	43.9 seconds	OCTOBER 21, 1964
7.	BARBARA FERRELL, MILDRETTA NETTER, WYOMIA TYUS, MARGRET BAILES	43.4 seconds	OCTOBER 19, 1968
8.	BARBARA FERRELL, MILDRETTA NETTER WYOMIA TYUS, MARGRET BAILES	42.8 seconds	OCTOBER 20, 1968

AMERICAN RECORDS—MEN'S TRACK
(as of March 1993)

100 Meters

Runner	Time	Date
Carl Lewis	9.86 seconds (world record)	Tokyo, Japan August 25, 1991

200 Meters

Runner	Time	Date
Carl Lewis	19.75 seconds	Indianapolis, Indiana June 19, 1983
Joe Deloach	19.75 seconds	Seoul, Korea September 28, 1988

400 Meters

Runner	Time	Date
Butch Reynolds	43.29 seconds (WR)	Zurich, Switzerland August 17, 1988

800 Meters

Runner	Time	Date
Johnny Gray	1:42.60 minutes	Koblenz, Germany August 28, 1985

110-Meter Hurdles

Roger Kingdom

12.92 seconds (WR)

Zurich, Switzerland,
August 16, 1989

800-Meter Relay

Leroy Burrell, Mike Marsh
Floyd Heard, Carl Lewis

1:19.11 minutes (WR)

Philadelphia, Pennsylvania
April 24, 1992

4 × 400-Meter Relay

Vince Matthews, Larry James
Ron Freeman, Lee Evans

2:56.16 minutes (WR)

Mexico City, Mexico,
October 20, 1968

4 × 400-Meter Relay

Steve Lewis, Danny Everett,
Kevin Robinzine, Butch Reynolds

2:56.16 minutes (WR)

Seoul, Korea,
October 1, 1988

4 × 800-Meter Relay

Santa Monica Track Club—
James Robinson, Earl Jones
David Mack, Johnny Gray

7:06.5 minutes

Walnut, California
April 26, 1986

Long Jump

Mike Powell

29 feet, 4½ inches (WR)

Tokyo, Japan
August 30, 1991

Triple Jump

Willie Banks

58 feet, 11½ inches

Indianapolis, Indiana
June 26, 1985

AMERICAN RECORDS—WOMEN'S TRACK
(as of March 1993)

100 Meters

Runners	Time	Date
Florence Griffith-Joyner	10.49 seconds (WR)	Indianapolis, Indiana, July 16, 1988

200 Meters

Florence Griffith-Joyner	21.34 seconds (WR)	Seoul, Korea, September 29, 1988

400 Meters

Valerie Brisco-Hooks	48.83 seconds	Los Angeles, California August 6, 1984

100-Meter Hurdles

Gail Devers-Roberts	12.48 seconds	Berlin, Germany September 10, 1991

National Team—400-Meter Relay

Diane Williams, Alice Brown Pam Marshall, Florence Griffith	41.55 seconds	Berlin, Germany August 21, 1987

800-Meter Relay

Louisiana State University Esther Jones, Tananjalyn Stanley, Dawn Sowell, Sylvania Brydson	1:32.57 minutes	Des Moines, Iowa April 28, 1989

4 × 400-Meter Relay

Diane Dixon, Denean Howard, Florence Griffith Joyner, Valerie Brisco	3:15.51 minutes	Seoul, Korea October 1, 1988

Long Jump

Jackie Joyner-Kersee	24 feet, 5½ inches	Indianapolis, Indiana August 13, 1987

Reference Section

Heptathlon

Jackie Joyner-Kersee	7291 points (WR)	Seoul, Korea
		September 23 & 24, 1988

AFRICAN-AMERICANS INDUCTED INTO THE NATIONAL TRACK & FIELD HALL OF FAME

Men's Track & Field

Name	Year Inducted	Event
Dave Albritton	1980	high jump
Robert Beamon	1977	long jump
Greg Bell	1988	long jump
Ralph Boston	1974	long jump
Lee Caloun	1974	110-meter hurdles
Milt Campbell	1989	decathlon
William Davenport	1982	110-meter hurdles
Harrison Dillard	1974	100-meter dash; 400-meter relay
Charles Dumas	1990	400-meter dash; 1600-meter relay
Lee Evans	1983	100-meter dash; 200-meter relay
Barney Ewell	1986	100-meter dash; 200-meter relay
Robert Hayes	1976	100-meter dash; 400-meter relay
Jim Hines	1979	100 meters; 400-meter relay
William DeHart Hubbard	1979	long jump
Rafer Johnson	1974	decathlon
Hayes Jones	1976	110-meter hurdles
Ralph Metcalfe	1975	100 meters; 200 meters
Jesse Owens	1974	100 meters; 200 meters
		200-meter relay, long jump
Eulace Peacock	1987	100 meters
Tommie Smith	1978	200 meters
Andrew Stanfield	1977	200 meters
John Thomas	1985	high jump
Eddie Tolan	1982	100 meters, 200 meters
Mal Whitfield	1974	800-meter run, 1600-meter relay
John Woodruff	1978	800 meters

Women's Track & Field

Name	Year Inducted	Event
Alice Coachman	1975	high jump
Mae Faggs	1976	400-meter relay
Barbara Ferrell	1988	400-meter relay
Nell Jackson	1989	not available
Madeline Manning	1984	800-meter run, 1600-meter relay
Mildred McDaniel	1983	high jump
Edith McGuire	1979	100-meter dash, 200-meter dash, 400-meter relay
Wyomia Tyus	1980	100-meter dash, 400-meter relay
Willye White	1981	long jump
Wilma Rudolph	1974	100-meter dash, 400-meter relay

Coaches

Coach	Year Inducted	College
Edward Hurt	1975	Morgan State University
Ed Temple	1989	Tennessee State University
Dr. Leroy Walker	1983	North Carolina Central University

AFRICAN-AMERICAN OLYMPIC MEDALISTS IN TRACK AND FIELD, 1948–1992

African-American Medalists: The XIVth Olympiad

	Medal	*Event*	*Time/Distance*
HARRISON DILLARD	gold	100–m dash	10.3 seconds, OR*
	gold	400–m relay	40.6 seconds
MAL WHITFIELD	gold	800–m run	1:49.2 minutes, OR
	gold	1600–m relay	3:10.4 minutes
NORWOOD EWELL	gold	400–m relay	40.6 seconds
	silver	100–m dash	10.4 seconds
LORENZO WRIGHT	gold	400–m relay	40.6 seconds
WILLIE STEELE	gold	long jump	25' 8"
ALICE COACHMAN	gold	high jump	5' 6", OR
AUDREY PATTERSON	bronze	200–m dash	25.2 seconds

*OR = Olympic Record

African-American Medalists: The XVth Olympiad

	Medal	Event	Time/Distance/Points
HARRISON DILLARD	gold	110-m hurdles	13.7 seconds, OR*
	gold	400-m relay	40.1 seconds
MAL WHITFIELD	gold	800-m run	1:49.2 minutes, OR
	silver	1600-m relay	3:04 minutes
ANDREW STANFIELD	gold	200-m dash	20.7 seconds, OR
	gold	400-m relay	40.1 seconds
JEROME BIFFLE	gold	long jump	24' 10"
MAE FAGGS	gold	400-m relay	45.9 seconds, OR
CATHERINE HARDY	gold	400-m relay	45.9 seconds, OR
BARBARA JONES	gold	400-m relay	45.9 seconds, OR
MEREDITH GOURDINE	silver	long jump	24' 8¼"
MILTON CAMPBELL	silver	decathlon	7,132 points
OLLIE MATSON	silver	1600-m relay	3:04 minutes
	bronze	400-m run	46.8 seconds

*OR = Olympic Record

African-American Medalists: The XVIth Olympiad

	Medal	Event	Time/Distance/Points
LEE CALHOUN	gold	110-m hurdles	13.5 seconds, OR*
MILDRED McDANIEL	gold	high jump	5' 9-1/4", OR, WR
CHARLES DUMAS	gold	high jump	6' 11-1/4", OR
MILTON CAMPBELL	gold	decathlon	7,708 points
GREG BELL	gold	long jump	25' 8-1/4"
LOU JONES	gold	1600-m relay	3:04.8 minutes
CHARLES JENKINS	gold	1600-m relay	3:04.8 minutes
	gold	400-m run	46.7 seconds
IRA MURCHISON	gold	400-m relay	39.5 seconds, OR, WR
LEAMON KING	gold	400-m relay	39.5 seconds, OR
RAFER JOHNSON	silver	decathlon	7,568 points
ANDREW STANFIELD	silver	200-m dash	20.7 seconds
WILLYE WHITE	silver	long jump	19' 11-3/4"
JOSH CULBREATH	bronze	400-m hurdles	51.6 seconds
MAE FAGGS	bronze	400-m relay	44.9 seconds
MARGRET MATTHEWS	bronze	400-m relay	44.9 seconds
WILMA RUDOLPH	bronze	400-m relay	44.9 seconds
ISABELLE DANIELS	bronze	400-m relay	44.9 seconds

*OR = Olympic Record, WR = World Record

African-American Medalists: The XVIIth Olympiad

	Medal	Event	Time/Distance/Points
RAFER JOHNSON	gold	decathlon	8,001 points, OR*
RALPH BOSTON	gold	long jump	26' 7-1/2", OR
LEE CALHOUN	gold	110-m hurdles	13.8 seconds
OTIS DAVIS	gold	400-m dash	44.9 seconds, OR, WR
	gold	1600-m relay	3:02.2 minutes, OR, WR
WILMA RUDOLPH	gold	100-M dash	11 seconds
	gold	200-m dash	24 seconds
	gold	400-m relay	44.5 seconds
MARTHA HUDSON	gold	400-m relay	44.5 seconds
LUCINDA WILLIAMS	gold	400-m relay	44.5 seconds
BARBARA JONES	gold	400-m relay	44.5 seconds
WILLIE MAY	silver	110-m hurdles	13.8 seconds
LESTER CARNEY	silver	200-m dash	20.6 seconds
IRVIN ROBERSON	silver	long jump	26' 7-1/4"
HAYES JONES	bronze	110-m hurdles	14 seconds
JOHN THOMAS	bronze	high jump	7' 1/4"
EARLENE BROWN	bronze	shot put	53' 10-1/4"

*OR = Olympic Record, WR = World Record

African-American Medalists: The XVIIIth Olympiad

	Medal	Event	Time/Distance
BOB HAYES	gold	100-m dash	10 seconds, OR, WR*
	gold	400-m relay	39 seconds, OR, WR
HENRY CARR	gold	200-m dash	20.3 seconds, OR
	gold	1600-m relay	3:00.7 minutes, OR, WR
PAUL DRAYTON	gold	400-m relay	39 seconds, OR, WR
	silver	200-m dash	20.5 seconds
HAYES JONES	gold	110-m hurdles	13.6 seconds
ULIS WILLIAMS	gold	1600-m relay	3:00.7 minutes, OR, WR
RICHARD STEBBINS	gold	400-m relay	39 seconds, OR, WR

	Medal	Event	Time/Distance/Points
WYOMIA TYUS	gold	100-m dash	11.4 seconds
	silver	400-m relay	43.9 seconds
EDITH McGUIRE	gold	200-m dash	23 seconds, OR
	silver	100-m dash	11.6 seconds
	silver	400-m relay	43.9 seconds
WILLYE WHITE	silver	400-m relay	43.9 seconds
MARILYN WHITE	silver	400-m relay	43.9 seconds
JOHN THOMAS	silver	high jump	7' 1-3/4"
RALPH BOSTON	silver	long jump	26' 4"
JOHN RAMBO	bronze	high jump	7' 1"

*OR = Olympic Record, WR = World Record

African-American Medalists: The XIXth Olympiad

	Medal	Event	Time/Distance
BOB BEAMON	gold	long jump	29' 2½", OR, WR*
JAMES HINES	gold	100-m dash	9.9 seconds, OR, WR
	gold	400-m relay	38.2 seconds, OR, WR
LEE EVANS	gold	400-m dash	43.8 seconds, OR, WR
	gold	1600-m relay	2:56.1 minutes, OR, WR
TOMMIE SMITH	gold	200-m dash	19.8 seconds, OR, WR
WILLIE DAVENPORT	gold	110-m hurdles	13.3 seconds, OR
CHARLES GREENE	gold	400-m relay	38.2 seconds, OR, WR
	bronze	100-m dash	10 seconds
RONNIE SMITH	gold	400-m relay	38.2 seconds, OR, WR
MELVIN PENDER	gold	400-m relay	38.2 seconds, OR, WR
RON FREEMAN	gold	1600-m relay	2:56.1 minutes, OR, WR
	bronze	400-m dash	44.4 seconds
VINCENT MATTHEWS	gold	1600-m relay	2:56.1 minutes, OR, WR
LARRY JAMES	gold	1600-m relay	2:56.1 minutes, OR, WR

	Medal	Event	Time/Distance/Points
	silver	400-m dash	43.9 seconds
WYOMIA TYUS	gold	100-m dash	11 seconds, OR, WR
	gold	400-m relay	42.8 seconds, OR, WR
BARBARA FERRELL	gold	400-m relay	42.8 seconds, OR, WR
	silver	100-m dash	11.1 seconds
MARGARET BAILES	gold	400-m relay	42.8 seconds, OR, WR
MADELINE MANNING	gold	800-m run	2:00.9 minutes, OR
MILDRETTE NETTER	gold	400-m relay	42.8 seconds, OR, WR
ERVIN HALL	silver	110-m hurdles	13.4 seconds
EDWARD CARUTHERS	silver	high hump	7' 3½"
JOHN CARLOS	bronze	200-m dash	20.0 seconds
RALPH BOSTON	bronze	long jump	26' 9¼"

*OR = Olympic Record, WR = World Record

African-American Medalists: The XXth Olympiad

	Medal	Event	Time/Distance
VINCENT MATTHEWS	gold	400-m run	44.66 seconds
ROD MILBURN	gold	110m-hurdles	13.24 seconds, OR, WR*
RANDY WILLIAMS	gold	long jump	27' ¼"
ROBERT TAYLOR	gold	400-m relay	38.19 seconds, OR, WR
	silver	100-m dash	10.24 seconds
LARRY BLACK	gold	400-m relay	38.19 seconds, OR, WR
	silver	200-m dash	20.19 seconds
EDDIE HART	gold	400-m relay	38.19 seconds, OR, WR
GERALD TINKER	gold	400-m relay	38.19 seconds, OR, WR
MADELINE MANNING	silver	1600-m relay	3:25.2 minutes
MABLE FERGUSON	silver	1600-m relay	3:25.2 minutes
CHERYL TOUSSAINT	silver	1600-m relay	3:25.2 minutes
WAYNE COLLETT	silver	400-m dash	44.80 seconds
ARNIE ROBINSON	bronze	long jump	26' 4"

*OR = Olympic Record, WR = World Record

African-American Medalists: The XXIst Olympiad

	Medal	Event	Time/Distance
ARNIE ROBINSON	gold	long jump	27' 4-3/4"
EDWIN MOSES	gold	400-meter hurdles	47.64 seconds, OR, WR*
MILLARD HAMPTON	gold	400-meter relay	38.33 seconds
	silver	200-meter dash	20.29 seconds
STEVE RIDDICK	gold	400-meter relay	38.33 seconds
HARVEY GLANCE	gold	400-meter relay	38.33 seconds
JOHN JONES	gold	400-meter relay	38.33 seconds
HERMAN FRAZIER	gold	1600-meter relay	2:58.7 minutes
	bronze	400-meter dash	44.95 seconds
BENNY BROWN	gold	1600-meter relay	2:58.7 minutes
MAXIE PARKS	gold	1600-meter relay	2:58.7 minutes
FRED NEWHOUSE	gold	1600-meter relay	2:58.7 minutes
	silver	400-meter dash	44.40 seconds
RANDY WILLIAMS	silver	long jump	26' 7-1/4"
JAMES BUTTS	silver	triple jump	56' 8-1/2"
ROSALYN BRYANT	silver	1600-meter relay	3:22.8 minutes
SHEILA INGRAM	silver	1600-meter relay	3:22.8 minutes
PAMELA JILES	silver	1600-meter relay	3:22.8 minutes
DEBRA SAPENTER	silver	1600-meter relay	3:22.8 minutes
DWAYNE EVANS	bronze	200-meter dash	20.43 seconds
WILLIE DAVENPORT	bronze	110-meter hurdles	13.38 seconds

*OR = Olympic Record, WR = World Record

African-American Medalists: The XXIInd Olympiad

U.S. boycotted games in Moscow.

African-American Medalists: The XXIIIrd Olympiad

	Medal	Event	Time/Distance/Points
CARL LEWIS	gold	100-m dash	10.97 seconds
	gold	200-m dash	19.80 seconds, OR*
	gold	long jump	8.54 meters
	gold	400-m relay	37.83 seconds, OR, WR
ALONZO BABERS	gold	400-m run	44.27 seconds
	gold	1600-m relay	2:57.91 minutes
ROGER KINGDOM	gold	110-m hurdles	13.20 seconds
EDWIN MOSES	gold	400-m hurdles	47.75 seconds
AL JOYNER	gold	triple jump	17.26 meters

	Medal	Event	Time/Distance/Points
SAM GRADDY	gold	400-m relay	37.83 seconds, OR, WR
	silver	100-m dash	10.19 seconds
RON BROWN	gold	400-m relay	37.83 seconds, OR, WR
CALVIN SMITH	gold	400-m relay	37.83 seconds, OR, WR
SUNDER NIX	gold	1600-m relay	2:57.91 minutes
RAY ARMSTEAD	gold	1600-m relay	2:57.91 minutes
ANTONIO McKAY	gold	1600-m relay	2:57.91 minutes
	bronze	400-m run	44.71 seconds
EVELYN ASHFORD	gold	100-m dash	10.97 seconds, OR
	gold	400-m relay	41.65 seconds
VALERIE BRISCO-HOOKS	gold	200-m dash	21.81 seconds, OR
	gold	400-m run	48.83 seconds, OR
	gold	1600-m run	3:18.29 minutes, OR
BENITA FITZGERALD-BROWN	gold	100-m hurdles	12.84 seconds
ALICE BROWN	gold	400-m relay	41.65 seconds
	silver	100-m dash	11.13 seconds
JEANETTE BOLDEN	gold	400-m relay	41.65 seconds
CHANDRA CHEESEBOROUGH	gold	400-m relay	41.65 seconds
	gold	1600-m relay	3:18.29 minutes, OR
	silver	400-m run	49.05 seconds
SHERRI HOWARD	gold	1600-m relay	3:18.29 minutes, OR
LILLIE LEATHERWOOD	gold	1600-m relay	3:18.29 minutes, OR
KIRK BAPTISTE	silver	200-m dash	19.96 seconds
GREG FOSTER	silver	110-m hurdles	13.23 seconds
DANNY HARRIS	silver	400-m hurdles	48.13 seconds
MIKE CONLEY	silver	triple jump	17.18 meters
FLORENCE GRIFFITH	silver	200-m dash	22.04 seconds
JUDI BROWN	silver	400-m hurdles	55.20 seconds
JACKIE JOYNER	silver	heptathlon	6,385 points
EARL JONES	bronze	800-run	1:43.83 minutes
KIM TURNER	bronze	100-m hurdles	13.06 seconds

*OR = Olympic Record, WR = World Record

African-American Medalists: The XXIVth Olympiad

XXIV Olympiad

Name	*Medal*	*Event*	*Time/Distance/Points*
CARL LEWIS	gold	100-m	9.92 seconds WR
	gold	long jump	28 ft. 7¼ inches
	silver	200-m	19.79 seconds
JOE DELOACH	gold	200-m	19.75 seconds OR
STEVE LEWIS	gold	400-m	43.87 seconds
	gold	4 × 400-m relay	2:56.16 minutes—tied WR
ROGER KINGDOM	gold	110-m hurdles	12.98 seconds OR
DANNY EVERETT	gold	4 × 400-m relay	2:56.16 minutes—tied WR
HAROLD "BUTCH" REYNOLDS	gold	4 × 400-m relay	2:56.16 minutes—tied WR
	silver	400-m	43.93 seconds
ANDRE PHILLIPS	gold	400-m hurdles	47.19 seconds OR
MIKE POWELL	silver	long jump	27 ft. 10¼ inches
ANTHONY CAMPBELL	bronze	110-m hurdles	13.38 seconds
EDWIN MOSES	bronze	400-m hurdles	47.56 seconds

Women's Track & Field

Name	*Medal*	*Event*	*Time/Distance/Points*
FLORENCE GRIFFITH-JOYNER	gold	100-m	10.54 WR
	gold	200-m	21.34 WR
	gold	4 × 100-m relay	41.98
	silver	4 × 400-m relay	3:15.51 minutes
JACKIE JOYNER-KERSEE	gold	heptathlon	7291 points WR
	gold	long jump	24 ft. 3¼ inches OR
EVELYN ASHFORD	gold	4 × 100-m relay	41.98
ALICE BROWN	gold	4 × 100-m relay	41.98
SHEILA ECHOLS	gold	4 × 100-m relay	41.98
DENEAN HOWARD	silver	4 × 400-m relay	3:15.51 minutes
DIANE DIXON	silver	4 × 400-m relay	3:15.51 minutes
VALERIE BRISCO	silver	4 × 400-m relay	3:15.51 minutes

African-American Medalists: The XXVth Olympiad

XXV Olympiad

Name	*Medal*	*Event*	*Time/Distance/Points*
MIKE MARSH	gold	200-m	20.01 seconds
	gold	4 × 100-m relay	37.40 seconds WR*
QUINCY WATTS	gold	400-m	43.50 seconds OR
		4 × 400-m relay	2:55.74 minutes WR*
KEVIN YOUNG	gold	400-m hurdles	46.78 seconds WR*

Name	Medal	Event	Time/Distance/Points
DENNIS MITCHELL	gold	4 × 100-m relay	37.40 seconds WR*
	bronze	100-m	10.04 seconds
LEROY BURRELL	gold	4 × 100-m relay	37.40 seconds WR*
CARL LEWIS	gold	4 × 100-m relay	37.40 seconds WR*
	gold	long jump	28 ft. 5½ inches
ANDREW YALMON	gold	4 × 400-m relay	2:55.74 minutes WR*
MICHAEL JOHNSON	gold	4 × 400-m relay	2:55.74 minutes WR*
MIKE CONLEY	gold	triple jump	59 ft. 7½ inches
STEVE LEWIS	gold	4 × 400-m relay	2:55.74 minutes WR*
	silver	400-m	44.21 seconds
TONY DEES	silver	110-m hurdles	13.24 seconds
MIKE POWELL	silver	long jump	28 ft. 4¼ inches
CHARLES SIMPKINS	silver	triple jump	57 ft. 9 inches
MIKE BATES	bronze	200-m	20.38 seconds
JOHNNY GRAY	bronze	800-m	1:43.97 minutes
JOE GREENE	bronze	long jump	27 ft. 4½ inches

*pending

Women's Track & Field

Name	Medal	Event	Time/Distance/Points
GAIL DEVERS	gold	100-m	10.82 seconds
GWEN TORRENCE	gold	200-m	21.81 seconds
	gold	4 × 100-m relay	42.11 seconds
	silver	4 × 400-m relay	3:20.92 minutes
JACKIE JOYNER-KERSEE	gold	heptathlon	7044 points
	bronze	long jump	23 ft. 2½ inches
ESTHER JONES	gold	4 × 100-m relay	42.11 seconds
CARLETTE GUIDRY	gold	4 × 100-m relay	42.11 seconds
EVELYN ASHFORD	gold	4 × 100-m relay	42.11 seconds
LAVONA MARTIN	silver	100-m hurdles	12.69 seconds
NATASHA KAISER	silver	4 × 400-m relay	3:20.92 minutes
JEARL MILES	silver	4 × 400-m relay	3:20.92 minutes
ROCHELLE STEVENS	silver	4 × 400-m relay	3:20.92 minutes
SANDRA FARMER-PATRICK	silver	400-m hurdles	53.69 seconds
JANEENE VICKERS	silver	400-m hurdles	54.31 seconds

OUTSTANDING AFRICAN-AMERICANS IN COLLEGE TRACK & FIELD
(1919–1945)

Boston University
Boston, Massachusetts 02215

Outstanding Athletes

Wharton, Clifton[1]
Franklin, Benjamin[2]

[1] Wharton, Clifton—captain on the 1921 Boston University team
[2] Franklin, Benjamin—captain on the 1938 Boston University team

Cornell University
Ithaca, New York 14851

All-American

Robeson, Jr., Paul[1] 1944

[1] Robeson, Jr., Paul—Honorable Mention: 1946 IC4A Indoor High Jump Champion; also played left end and place kicker in football

Howard University
Washington, D.C. 20059

Coaches of Varsity Teams

Morrison, Edward 1920–23
Watson, Louis 1924–25
West, Charles 1926–27
Verdell, Tom 1930
Burr, John C. 1936–38
Payne, Harry 1938
Chase, 1942

Marquette University
Milwaukee, Wisconsin 53233

Outstanding Athletes

Metcalfe, Ralph[1]

[1] Metcalfe, Ralph—member of the 1936 United States Olympic team

Ohio State University
Columbus, Ohio 43210-1166

All-American

Owens, Jesse[1] 1936
Albritton, David[2] 1936–38
Walker, Melvin—HJ 1936

[1] Owens, Jesse—member of the 1936 United States Olympic track and field team
[2] Albritton, David—High Jump; winner of three NCAA titles; member of the 1936 United States Olympic track and field team

Temple University
Philadelphia, Pennsylvania 19122

Outstanding Athletes

Peacock, Eulace[1]
Threadgill, Albert[2]

[1] Peacock, Eulace—competed for Temple University 1935–38; broad jump
[2] Threadgill, Albert—competed for Temple University 1937–38; high jump

Tennessee State University
Nashville, Tennessee 37203

Coach of Varsity Team

Harris, Tom 1945–46

University of Colorado
Boulder, Colorado 80309

Other Outstanding Athletes

Croter, Gill[1]
Walton, Claude[2]

[1] Croter, Gill—competed in track, 1936
[2] Walton, Claude—compete in track, 1937

University of Michigan
Ann Arbor, Michigan 48109

All-American

Hubbard, William Dehart[1] 1924
Tolan, Thomas "Eddie"[2] 1932

Other Outstanding Athletes

Brooks, Booker
Ward, Willis

[1] Hubbard, William Dehart—member of the 1924 United States Olympic track and field team; the first black American to win a Gold Medal in the Olympics
[2] Tolan, Thomas "Eddie"—member of the 1932 United States Olympic track and field team

University of Oregon
Eugene, Oregon 97403

All Pacific Coast

Robinson, Robert—NDC, PV 1929
Robinson, Mack—BJ, PCC 1938
Browning, Allen—NDC, 100/200 YD 1943

All-American

Robinson, Mack[1] 1938

[1] Robinson, Mack—1938 NCAA champion, 200-meter dash; member of the 1936 United States Olympic track and field team

University of Pennsylvania
Philadelphia, Pennsylvania 19104

Outstanding Athletes

Jones, Ed[1]
Rogers, C. Dewey[2]
Granger, Lloyd[3]
Alexander, Raymond P.[4]

[1] Jones, Ed—ran track from 1919 to 1921
[2] Rogers, C. Dewey—ran track from 1919 to 1921
[3] Granger, Lloyd—ran track from 1919 to 1921
[4] Alexander, Raymond P.—ran track from 1920

University of Pittsburgh
Pittsburgh, Pennsylvania 15213

Outstanding Athletes

Woodruff, John Y.[1]

[1] Woodruff, John Y.—member of the 1936 United States Olympic track and field team

West Virginia State College
Institute, West Virginia 25112

Coach of Varsity Teams

Barnette, Leonard 1924–25

OUTSTANDING AFRICAN-AMERICANS IN COLLEGE TRACK AND FIELD (1946–1992)
BY CONFERENCE

MISSOURI VALLEY CONFERENCE

1. Wichita State University
2. University of Tulsa
3. Indiana State University
4. Creighton University
5. Drake University

6. Southern Illinois University
7. West Texas State University
8. Southwest Missouri State University
9. Illinois State University
10. Bradley University

Wichita State University
Wichita, Kansas 67208–0018

Coaches of Varsity Teams

Foote, Cyril (Assistant), 1985

All Missouri Valley Conference

Person, Roy, CC, 1967
Pratt, Nate, LJ, 1968–69
Carrington, Preston, LJ, 1971–72

All-American

Carrington, Preston, LJ, 1971–72

Creighton University
Omaha, Nebraska 68178

Other Outstanding Athletes

Gibson, Robert[1]

[1] Gibson, Robert—competed in basketball and baseball

Drake University
Des Moines, Iowa 50311

All-American

Drew, Howard, 1912
Ford, Jim, 1951
Betton, Arnold, 1952
Durant, Charles, 1961
Martin, Sterling, 1985

Women's Track

Blackman, Carlon, 1983

Other Outstanding Athletes

Nolan, George
Harris, James A.
Durant, Charles

Women's Track

Pulliam, Dolph

Southern Illinois University
Carbondale, Illinois 62901

All-American

Dupree, Jim, 1960s
Moore, Oscar, 1960s
Crockett, Ivory, 1971

Southern Illinois University's Hall of Fame

Payton, Eugene[1]
Dupree, Jim
Crockett, Ivory

Other Outstanding Athletes

Benson, Charles
Brown, Lonnie
Lee, David
Rock, Rick
Duncan, Parry
Geary, Randy
Robins, Phil
Franks, Michael
Wray, Stephen

[1] Payton, Eugene—first black American to earn a letter at Southern Illinois University

SUN BELT CONFERENCE

1. University of South Alabama
2. Old Dominion University
3. Jacksonville University
4. University of North Carolina, Charlotte
5. University of New Orleans
6. Western Kentuck

7. Louisiana Tech
8. Lamar University
9. University of Arkansas, Little Rock
10. Arkansas State University
11. University of Southwestern Louisiana
12. Virginia Commonwealth University

Louisiana Tech University
Ruston, Louisiana 71272

All Southland Conference

Thornton, George, OD HJ 1973
Smith, Wesley, OD LJ 1974–75
Ford, Monroe, OD LJ 1976
Woods, Wendell, LJ 1978
Webb, Darrell, HJ 1980
Garrett, Cornell, 100M 1981
Holman, Victor, ID HH 1981
Webb, Darrell, ID HJ 1981

Lamar University
Beaumont, Texas 77710

All Southland Conference

LeBlac, Joe, 1964
Gipson, Efren "De De," 1973–74
Harris, Jackie, MR
Nichols, Jerry, MR 1984
Amboree, Troy, MR 1984

BIG WEST CONFERENCE
(Pacific Coast Athletic Association until 1988)

1. University of Nevada, Las Vegas
2. University of California, Irvine
3. California State University, Long Beach
4. New Mexico State University
5. California State University, Fullerton

6. San Jose State University
7. University of California, Santa Barbara
8. University of Pacific
9. Utah State University

University of California, Irvine
Irvine, California 92717

Coaches of Varsity Teams

Men's Track and Field/Cross Country
Roberson, Bo (Head), 1971–72

Women's Track and Field
Williams, Dan (Head), 1982–89

All Pacific Coast Athletic Association

King, La Monte, 100M, 200M, LJ 1978–79
Chambers, Tim, 400MR, MR 1979
McGee, Darryl, 400MR, MR 1979
Frazier, Thomas, 800M, MR 1979–80

Kidd, Carlysle, 400M, MR 1979–81
Wells, Tony, 400M, MR 1979–81
Corrin, Michael, LJ 1980
Chapman, Phil, HJ 1981
Carey, Ed, 200M, 400M, MR 1981–82
Holliday, Rick, TJ 1983
Powell, Michael, 400MR, HJ 1984
Todd, Harold, 400MR 1984
Clark, Selwyn, 400MR 1984

Other Outstanding Athletes

Women's Track
Westbrook, Brenda
Kelley, Michelle
Stanford, Carole

Reference Section

San Jose State University
San Jose, California 95192-0062

Coaches of Varsity Teams

Livers, Larry (Assistant), 1972–80
Poynter, Robert (Assistant), 1980–90

All-American

Wyatt, Herman, 1952–53
Norton, Ray, 1958–59
Poynter, Robert, 1959
Williams, Errol, 1959–60
Compton, Maurice, 1966
Herman, Wayne, 1966

Smith, Tommie, 1966–68
Evans, Lee, 1968–69
Davis, Sam, 1968–69
Anderson, Marion, 1969
Clayton, Kirk, 1969
Smith, Ronnie Ray, 1969
Carty, George, 1969–71
Whitaker, Ron, 1975
Livers, Ron, 1975, 1977–78
Cooper, Dedy, 1976–77
Prince, Cleve, 1981
Thomas, Ken, 1981
Green, Dwayne, 1981
Torrence, Virgil, 1981
Holloway, Bernie, 1982

WESTERN ATHLETIC CONFERENCE

1. University of Wyoming
2. University of Utah
3. University of Texas at El Paso
4. San Diego State University
5. Colorado State University

6. University of New Mexico
7. Fresno State University
8. University of Hawaii
9. Air Force Academy

University of Wyoming
Laramie, Wyoming 82071

All Western Athletic Conference

Robinson, Herman, 1964
Washington, Vic, 1967
Johnson, Huey, 1969
Frazier, Michael, 1969
Jones, Arabia, 1971
Black, Robert, 1974
Benhom, Ben, 1974
Kyle, Aaron, 1975
Williams, Gladstone, 1978
White, Michael, 1980
Bennett, James, 1987

Women's Track

Johnson, Tanya, 1976
Bradley, Jeannette, 1980
Miller, Pat, 1980

Western Athletic Conference

Bennett, James, 1987

University of Texas, El Paso
El Paso, Texas 79968

All Western Athletic Conference

Jackson, Harrington J.J.,[1] 1970–72
Deal, Jerome,[2] 1978–81
Scott, Carlos, 1980

All-American

Beamon, Robert,[3] 1967–68
Turner, Kim,[4] 1983–84

[1] Jackson, Harrington J.J.—1972 Western Athletic Conference 100-Meter Dash Champion
[2] Deal, Jerome—1981 Western Athletic Conference 100-Meter Dash Champion
[3] Beamon, Robert—1967 NCAA Indoor Long Jump Champion; member of the 1968 United States Olympic Track Team
[4] Turner, Kim—1984 NCAA 100-Meter Hurdle champion; member of the 1984 United States Olympic Track Team

San Diego State University
San Diego, California 92182

All-American

Steele, William,[1] LJ, 1947–48
Williams, Wes, 440/IH, 1969–70
Robinson, Arnie,[2] LJ, 1970–71
Williams, Steve, 100M, 1974
Wheeler, Quentin,[3] 400M, 1976

Other Outstanding Athletes

Blaylock, Chris, 100M
McDonald, Brad, 200M
Almbruster, Michael, 800M
Robinson, Earl, 1500M
Martin, Otis, 500M
Shy, Don, 110MH

Discus Throw

Ridge, Houston

Women's Track

Taylor, Anovia, 100M
Smith, Lori, 100MLJ
Sheffield, Lantanya, 100M
Chambers, Rene, 200M, 400M
Bryson, Yolanda, 110MH

Bullard, Yvette, 400M
Charles, Donna, 400M

[1] Steele, William—member of the 1948 United States Olympic Track and Field team
[2] Robinson, Arnie—member of the 1972 United States Olympic Track and Field team
[3] Wheeler, Quentin—member of the 1976 United States Olympic Track and Field team
[4] Gwynn, Chris—member of the 1984 United States Olympic Track and Field team

University of New Mexico
Albuquerque, New Mexico 87131

All-American

Howard, Richard, 440MH 1959
Plummer, Adolph, 440YD 1961
Kennedy, Larry, 660YD 1964
Robinson, Clarence, LJ 1965
Rivers, Bernie, 400YR 1966
Matison, Rene, 440YR 1966
Robinson, Ira, LJ 1966
Baxter, Art, TJ 1966–67
Mitchell, Clark, 660YD 1967
Solomon, Michael, 60YD 1977
Moore, Roger, 2-Min. R 1983
Rudd, Dwayne, LJ 1983–84

MID-AMERICAN CONFERENCE

1. Ohio University
2. University of Toledo
3. Miami University
4. Eastern Michigan University
5. Kent State University
6. Northern Illinois University
7. Western Michigan University
8. Bowling Green State University
9. Central Michigan University
10. Ball State University
11. University of Akron

Ohio University
Athens, Ohio 45701–2979

All Mid-American Conference

Mitchell, Daniel, 1962–63, 1965

All-American

Mitchell, Darnell, 800M 1965
Taylor, Emmett, 200M 1968

Other Outstanding Athletes

Perkis, Rupel A., 1950–51
Carney, Les[1], 1960

[1] Carney, Les—first black athlete from Ohio University to compete in the Olympics; member of the 1960 United States Olympic Track and Field Team

University of Toledo
Toledo, Ohio 43606

Coaches of Varsity Teams

Men's Track and Field
Jones, Eugene (Head)

Women's Track and Field
Kearney, Beverly (Head)

All Mid-American Conference
Harris, Byron, 1983–84

All-American
Hopkins, Aaron,[1] 1966–67

[1] Hopkins, Aaron—NCAA Indoor Champion

Miami University
Oxford, Ohio 45056

Coaches of Varsity Teams

Women's Track
Williams, Joselyn, 1982–84

All Mid-American Conference
Downing, Ted, 1967–68

All-American
Downing, Ted, 1968

Miami University's Hall of Fame
Downing, Ted

Eastern Michigan University
Ypsilanti, Michigan 48197

Eastern Michigan University's Hall of Fame
Jones, Hayes

Kent State University
Kent, Ohio 44242

Coaches of Varsity Teams

Men's and Women's Track and Field
Richburg, Orin (Head), 1978–93

All Mid-American Conference
Curry, Norman, HJ 1964–66
Richburg, Orin, 100M/200M 1967–69
Harris, Ted, 800M 1971
Turner, Len, 100M/200M 1971–72
Tinker, Gerald, 100M 1973
Gregory, Calvin, 400IH/110M HH 1975
Carter, Terry, 100M 1979
Thrist, Harrison, LJ 1980
Jefferson, Thomas, 100M/200M 1982–84

All-American
Hughes, Ron, ID 1965
Richburg, Orin, OD 1967
Tinker, Gerald, ID and OD 1973
Harris, Ted, ID 1973
Carter, Terry, ID 1979

Kent State University's Hall of Fame
Tinker, Gerald Alexander
Turner, Len
Richburg, Orin

Northern Illinois University
Dekalb, Illinois 60115

Coaches of Varsity Teams

Cross Country
Kimmons, Willie (Head)

Western Michigan University
Kalamazoo, Michigan 49008

All Mid-American Conference

Taylor, Ed, 1948
Murchinson, IRA, 1954, 1957–58
Skinner, Byron, 1955
Littlejohn, Alonzo, 1961–62
Johnson, Joel, 1962
Randolph, Tom, 1968–69
Pruitt, Terry, 1970
Rencher, Don, 1970
Gaines, Homer, 1972
Baker, Alan, 1974
White, Craig, 1974
Miles, Dana, 1974

Williams, Darrell, 1978
Lockhart, Michael, 1980
Hamilton, Carol, 1981–82
Ellis, Ian, 1982
Washington, Alex, 1983–84
Williams, James, 1983–84

All-American

Murchinson, Ira, 1957–58
Littlejohn, Alonzo, 1961
Randolph, Tom, 1968
Washington, Alex, 1983

Western Michigan University's Hall of Fame

Murchinson, Ira

SOUTHEASTERN CONFERENCE

1. University of Georgia
2. University of Kentucky
3. Mississippi State University
4. Vanderbilt University
5. University of Mississippi
6. Auburn University

7. University of Alabama
8. University of Tennessee
9. University of Florida
10. Louisiana State University
11. University of Arkansas
12. University of South Carolina

University of Georgia
Athens, Georgia 30613

All Southeastern Conference

Lattany, Mel,[1] 100M, 400MR, 60Y 1979–81
Christian, Clarence, 1980
Walker, Herschel, S, 400MR 1981–82
Simmons, Darryl, LJ 1982
Blalock, Stanley, 300MR 1984

Women's Track

Rankins, Kathy, LJ 1984

All-American

Lattany, Mel, 1980–81
Johnson, Paul, 1981
Richards, William, 110M HH 1981
Christian, Clarence, LJ 1982
Walker, Herschel, ID 60YH 1982

Women's Track

Rankin, Kenny, LJ 1984

[1] Lattany, Mel—member of the 1980 United States Olympic Track and Field Team; 400-Meter Relay; 1981 World University Games 100-Meter Champion; 1981 World Cup 200-Meter Champion

University of Kentucky
Lexington, Kentucky 40506-0019

All Southeastern Conference

Green, Jim, 1968–71
Mayes, Marvin, 1970
Lightsey, William, 1970
Grimes, Hamil, 1980

Women's Track and Field

Lowe, Tanya, 1983–84

All-American

Green, Jim, 1968
Mayes, Marvin, 1970
Grimes, Hamil, 1980

Mississippi State University
Mississippi State, Mississippi 39762

Coaches of Varsity Teams

White, Vernon (Assistant), 1976–78

All-American

Jennings, Elvis,[1] 1976
Washington, George,[2] 1982
Hadley, Michael[3]
Jones, Darryl[4]
Moore, Michael[5]

Other Outstanding Athletes

Whitelead, Les, HJ
Gray, Samuel, MR
Darby, Jimmy, LJ
Milsap, Leroy, TJ
Spane, Charles, R

[1] Jennings, Elvis—1976 NCAA 440-Yard Dash Champion
[2] Washington, George—member of the 440-Yard Relay Team
[3] Hadley, Michael—member of the 440-Yard Relay Team
[4] Jones, Darryl—member of the 440-Yard Relay Team
[5] Moore, Michael—member of the 440-Yard Relay Team

University of Mississippi
University, Mississippi 38677

All Southeastern Conference

Nelson, Nicky, 880 MR, ID 1983–84
Tate, Cornelius, 880 MR, ID 1984
Cartlidge, Perry, MR, ID 1984
Dean, Melvin, MR, ID 1984
Spry, Ralph, LJ, OD 1982–83
Daniel, Clarence, 400M OD 1983
Dees, Tony, 110HH OD 1983

All-American

Spry, Ralph, LJ 1982–83
Dees, Tony, 60HH 1983–84
Daniel, Clarence, 1983–84

Auburn University
Auburn University, Alabama 36849

All Southeastern Conference

Outlin, Cliff, 100YD 1974–75
Easley, Tony, 60YD, LJ 1976
Glance, Harvey, 100M, 60YD 1976–78
Walker, James, 60YHH, 110MHH, 400MH 1976–78
Smith, Willie, 440Y, 400M 1977–78
Strother, Steven, DMRT 1979
Floyd, Stanley, 100M, 60YD 1980
Miller, Eugene, 110MH 1980
Franklin, Byron, 1980

All-American

Outlin, Cliff, 1974–75
Easley, Tony, 1976
Glance, Harvey, 1976–77
Miller, Eugene, 1980
Franklin, Byron, 1980
Brooks, Larry, 1980
Brooks, Calvin, 1983–84

University of Tennessee
Knoxville, Tennessee 37901-9926

All-American

James, Sam, SC, 1979
Blair, Anthony, 400MD, 440YD 1979–80
Hancock, Anthony, LJ 1980
Miller, Michael, 60YD 1980
Gault, Willie, 100M HH, 60YH, 100MD, 110MH 1981–83
Towns, Reggie, 110MH 1983–84
Graddy, Sam, 100MD 1983–84
Wilson, Jerome, 110MH, 400MH

University of Florida
Gainesville, Florida 32604

All Southeastern Conference

Coleman, Ron, 1969–70, 1972
Jenkins, Nate, 1973
Brown, Beaufort, 1973–75
Bostic, Hesley, 1973–75
Rambo, Robert, 1974

Goings, Mitchell, 1974
Alexander, Winfred, 1974
Tuitt, Horace, 1976
Sharpe, Michael, 1976
Simmons, Palmer, 1976
Barriffe, Clive, 1976
Gray, Noel, 1976
Mayo, Wesley, 1977–78
Luckie, Dock, 1978–79
Pringle, Jim, 1979–80
Gray, Kenneth, 1980–81, 1983
Brown, Floyd, 1981
Miller, Hugo, 1981
Green, Rickey, 1981
Holmes, Stanley, 1981

Women's Track
Fowler, Oralee
Henry, Dee
Pitts, Alverretta
Bressant, Piper
Campbell, Donna
Lotmore, Sharon

All-American

Men's Track

Brown, Beaufort, 1973–75
Goings, Mitchell, 1974
Rambo, Robert, 1974
Alexander, Winfred, 1974–75
Sharpe, Michael, 1975
Gray, Noel, 1975
Tuitt, Horace, 1975–76
Barriffe, Clive, 1978
Pringle, Jim, 1978–79
Green, Ricky, 1980
Mattox, Cullen, 1980

Women's Track
Allwood, Rose
Ray, Lorraine
Ferguson, Shonell

Dunlap, Patty
Lewis, Lori
Rodgers, Pam
Pitts, Alverretta
Bressant, Piper
Mercer, Lori

University of Arkansas
Fayetteville, Arkansas 72701

Coaches of Varsity Teams

Redwine, Stanley (Hurdles, Sprints), 1985–93
Conley, Michael (Volunteer, Assistant), 1985–93

All-American

Conley, Michael, 1984–85
Boykins, Marlon, 400M, 800M 1992
Doakes, Ray, HJ 1992
French, Jimmy, 200M 1990–92
Henderson, Vincent, 100M 1992
Phillips, Chris, 35MH, 110MH 1992

University of South Carolina
Columbia, South Carolina 29208

All Metro Conference

Rhodes, Vernon, 200 and 400M 1984
Johnsson, Earl, Decathlon 1984
Taylor, Ollie, 100M 1984
Smith, Wayne, LJ 1984

All-American

Thomas, George, 1977
Adams, Rolando, 1979
Rambo, Tony, 1980
Kirkland, Gus, 1981

TRANS-AMERICAN CONFERENCE

1. Northwestern State University
2. Houston Baptist University
3. Centenary College

4. North Texas State University
5. Mercer University
6. Stetson University

Northwestern State University of Louisiana
Natchitoches, Louisiana 71497

All-American

Brown, Michael, LJ, NAIA 1973–76
Hardwell, Robert, 100 and 200M, NAIA 1976
McIntosh, Robert, TJ, NAIA 1976
Handy, Jarrot, TJ, LJ 1980
Oatis, Victor, 400MR, NC 1981
Delaney, Joe, 400MR, NC 1981
Johnson, Mario, 400MR, NC 1981
Brown, Ray, 400MR 1982
Washington, Edgar, 400MR 1982
Johnson, Mario, 400MR 1982
McGloory, Percy, 400MR 1984
Johnson, Mario, 400MR 1984
Washington, Edgar, 400MR 1984
Evans, Cedric, 400MR 1984

Houston Baptist University
Houston, Texas 77074

All Trans-America Athletic Conference

Thompson, Rick,[1] 1983

[1] Thompson, Rick—1983 NCAA Outdoor High Jump champion

North Texas State University
Denton, Texas 76203

Coaches of Varsity Teams

Brown, Abe

EAST COAST CONFERENCE

1. American University

2. Hofstra University

Hofstra University
Hempstead, Long Island 11550

Coaches of Varsity Teams

Jackson, John (Head)

WEST COAST CONFERENCE

1. University of San Francisco

2. Pepperdine University

University of San Francisco
San Francisco, California 94117

Other Outstanding Athletes

Matson, Ollie[1]

[1] Matson, Ollie—played on the 1950–51 University of San Francisco team; member of the 1952 United States Olympic Track and Field team

Pepperdine University
Malibu, California 90265

All West Coast Athletic Conference

Johnson, Bill, 1953–54
Walters, Jerome, 1956

All-American

Johnson, William, 1953–54
Walters, Jerome, 1956
Howard, Harold, 1964–65
Coleman, Norman, 1965
McNeil, Pablo, 1967–68

Women's Track

Brown, Terrezene, 1967
Charlton, Vilma, 1967
White, Marilyn,[1] 1967

Pepperdine University's Hall of Fame

Johnson, Bill
Walters, Jerome
Matson, Jr., Ollie

[1] White, Marilyn—member of the 1964 U.S. Olympic Track and Field team

MID-WESTERN CITY CONFERENCE

1. Detroit Mercy University
2. University of Evansville
3. Loyola University of Chicago
4. Oklahoma City University

BIG EAST CONFERENCE

1. Georgetown University
2. Providence College
3. University of Pittsburgh
4. University of Connecticut
5. Seton Hall University
6. Boston College
7. St. John's University
8. Villanova University
9. Syracuse University
10. University of Miami (Florida)

University of Pittsburgh
Pittsburgh, Pennsylvania 15213

Outstanding Athletes

Douglas, Herb[1]
Sowell, Arnold[2]
Utterback, Everett
Salter, Bryant
Barnwell, Mel
Farmer, Karl
King, Wes

[1] Douglas, Herb—member of the 1948 United States Olympic Track and Field Team
[2] Sowell, Arnold—member of the 1956 United States Olympic Track and Field Team

Seton Hall University
South Orange, New Jersey 07079

Coaches of Varsity Teams

Men's Track

Moon, John[1] (Head), 1970–1993
Knight, Melvin (Assistant), 1976–82

Presley, Ira (Assistant), 1977
Rogers, Earl (Assistant), 1982

Women's Track

Roman, Beverly (Assistant), 1983

All Eastern College Athletic Conference

Shepherd, Kenneth,[2] 1982
Denman, Brian, 400M ID 1982
Chambliss, Barron, 300M ID 1985

All-American

Fields, Benjamin F., 1976

Seton Hall University's Hall of Fame

Stanfield, Andrew[3]

[1] Moon, John—1975 *Coach and Athlete* magazine's Man of the Year; 1981 Big East Conference Coach of the Year
[2] Shepherd, Kenneth—member of the 400-Meter Relay Team
[3] Stanfield, Andrew—member of the 1952 United States Olympic Track and Field Team (200-Meter Gold Medalist); member of the 1956 United States Olympic Track and Field Team (200-Meter Silver Medalist)

St. John's University
Jamaica, New York 11439

Coaches of Varsity Teams

Davis, Ken (Assistant)

Other Outstanding Athletes

Fields, Carl[1]

[1] Fields, Carl—captain of the 1942 St. John's University team

Villanova University
Villanova, Pennsylvania 19085

Coaches of Varsity Teams

Men and Women's Track and Field and Cross Country

Jenkins, Dr. Charles (Head), 1981–90

Women's Track and Field

Raveling, George (Assistant), 1967–68
Littlepage, Craig (Assistant), 1973–75
Thompson, James (Head), 1973–83

Big East Champions

Wilson, Rodney—OD 110MHC, ID 55MHC 1981–83
Young, Carlton—OD 200MC, ID 400MC, OD 400MC 1982–83
Marshall, John—ID 800MC, ID 500MC 1983–84
Booker, Martin—OD 400MHC, OD 110MHC, ID 55MHC 1983–85
Valentine, Tony—OD 400MHC 1984

IC4A Champions

Jenkins, Charles—OD 440YC, ID 600YC 1955–57
Stead, Charles—ID HJC 1957–59
Reavis, Phil—ID HJC, OD HJC 1956–58
Collymore, Ed—ID 60YC, OD 220YC 1957–59
Joe, Billy—ID SPC, OD SPC 1961
Budd, Frank—ID 60YC, OD 100YC, OD 220YC 1960–62
Livers, Larry—OD 120YHC 1965
Hall, Erv—ID 60YC, OD 120YHC 1967–69

Other Outstanding Athletes

Jenkins, Charles,[1] 1955–57
Reavis, Phil,[2] 1958
Stead, Charles,[3] 1957–59
Collymore, Ed,[4] 1958–59

Budd, Frank,[5] 1961–62
Joe, Billy,[6] 1961
Livers, Larry,[7] 1965
Hall, Erv,[8] 1969
James, Larry,[9] 1969
Hymann, Lamonte,[10] 1971
Dale, Tim,[11] 1976–78
Cooper, Nate,[12] 1977–79
Brown, Keith,[13] 1979
Maree, Sydney,[14] 1979–81
Wilson, Rodney,[15] 1980–83
Young, Carlton,[16] 1983

[1] Jenkins, Charles—IC4A Outdoor 440-Yard Champion, IC4A Indoor 600-Yard Champion, member of the 1956 United States Olympic Track and Field Team (Gold Medalist)
[2] Reavis, Phil—NCAA High Jump Champion, IC4A Outdoor High Jump Champion; IC4A Indoor High Jump champion; member of the 1956 United States Olympic Track and Field Team
[3] Stead, Charles—IC4A Indoor High Jump Champion
[4] Collymore, Ed—NCAA 222-Yard Champion; IC4A outdoor 220-Yard Champion; 100-Yard Champion, IC4A Indoor 60-Yard champion
[5] Budd, Frank—NCAA Outdoor 100-Yard Champion; NCAA Outdoor 220-Yard Champion, IC4A Outdoor 100-Yard Champion, IC4A 220-Yard Champion, IC4A Indoor 60-Yard Champion
[6] Joe, Billy—IC4A Indoor Shot Put Champion; IC4A Outdoor Shot Put Champion
[7] Livers, Larry—IC4A Outdoor 120-Yard Hurdles Champion
[8] Hall, Erv—NCAA Outdoor 120-Yard Hurdle champion; IC4A Indoor 60-yard Championship; IC4A Outdoor 120-Yard Hurdle Champion; 100-Yard Champion; NCAA Indoor 60-Yard Champion
[9] James, Larry—NCAA 440-Yard Champion; IC4A Indoor 600-Yard Champion; IC4A Outdoor 400-Yard Champion, members of the 1968 United States Olympic Track and Field Team
[10] Hymann, Lamonte—IC4A Indoor 440-Yard Champion
[11] Dale, Tim—IC4A Outdoor 400-Meter Champion, IC4A Indoor 440-Yard Champion
[12] Cooper, Nate—IC4A Indoor Triple Jump Champion; IC4A Outdoor Triple Jump Champion
[13] Brown, Keith—IC4A Indoor 440-Yard Champion
[14] Maree, Sydney—IC4A Three-Mile Champion; NCAA Outdoor 5000M Champion; IC4A Outdoor 5000M Champion; IC4A Indoor 5000M Champion; NCAA Outdoor 1500M Champion; IC4A Indoor 3000M Champion; member of the 1984 United States Olympic Track and Field Team
[15] Wilson Rodney—NCAA Indoor 60-Yard Hurdles Champion; IC4A Outdoor 110-Meter Hurdles Champion; IC4A Indoor 55-Meter Hurdles Champion; Big East Conference Outdoor 110-Meter Hurdles Champion; Big East Conference Indoor 55-Meter Hurdles Champion
[16] Young, Carlton—NCAA Indoor 440-Yard Champion; IC4A Indoor 400-Meter Champion; Big East Conference, Outdoor 200-Meter Champion; Big East Conference, Outdoor 200-Meter Champion; Big East Conference, Indoor 400-Meter Champion; Big East Conference, Outdoor 400-Meter Champion

University of Miami (Florida)
Miami, Florida 33124

All-American

Copeland, Horace, 1991–92

BIG EIGHT CONFERENCE

1. Oklahoma State University
2. University of Nebraska
3. University of Colorado
4. Iowa State University

5. University of Oklahoma
6. Kansas State University
7. University of Kansas
8. University of Missouri

Oklahoma State University
Stillwater, Oklahoma 74078

All Big-Eight Conference

Hazley, Orlando,[1] 1959
Butler, James,[2] 1980

All-American

Butler, James,[3] 1980–81

Other Outstanding Athletes

Harris, Earl
Ingram, Ron
Blakely, Don

[1] Hazley, Orlando—220-Yard Dash Champion
[2] Butler, James—100-Yard and 200-Yard Dash Champion; 1980 Henry Schute Award recipient
[3] Butler, James—100 and 200-Yard Dash

University of Nebraska
Lincoln, Nebraska 68588-0123

All-American

Men's Track

Greene, Charles,[1] 1966–67
Lee, Jeff,[2] 1977

Women's Track

Murray, Normalee,[3] 1980–81
Ottey, Merlene,[4] 1980–82
McQueen, Alicia,[5] 1982
James, Debra,[6] 1982
Tate, Marcia,[7] 1982
Thacker, Angela,[8] 1982–83
Blanford, Rhonda,[9] 1982–83
Burke, Janet,[10] 1982–83
Powell, Debra, 1984
Ashmore, Holly, 1984
Smith, Heather, 1984

All Big-Eight Conference

Case, Garth,[11] 1969–70, 1972
Greene, Charles,[12] 1965–67

[1] Greene, Charles—NCAA Champion 60-Yard Dash (Indoor)
[2] Lee, Jeff—NCAA Champion 60-Yard High Hurdles (Indoor)
[3] Murray, Normalee—300-Meter Dash; 800-Meter Sprint Medley; 1600-Meter Relay
[4] Ottey, Merlene—300-Meter Dash; 200-Meter Dash; 800-Meter Spring Medley; 60-Yard Dash
[5] McQueen, Alicia—60-Yard Dash; 300-Yard Dash
[6] James, Debra—400-Meter Relay; 60-Yard Dash; 880-Yard Relay
[7] Tate, Marcia—600-Yard Run; Mile Relay
[8] Thacker, Angela—60-Yard Dash; Long Jump; 200-Meter Dash
[9] Blanford, Rhonda—60-Yard Hurdles; 880-Yard Relay; 100-Meter Hurdles
[10] Burke, Janet—60-Yard Run Champion
[11] Case, Garth—Indoor, 600-Yard Run Champion
[12] Greene, Charles—Outdoor, 100-Yard and 200-Yard Dash

University of Colorado
Boulder, Colorado 80309

Other Outstanding Athletes

Bolen, David—competed in track, 1948

Iowa State University
Ames, Iowa 50011

All Big-Eight Conference

Harris, Dan, 1984–85
Dixon, Leroy, 1985

All American

Men's Track

Carson, Steven, 1965–67
Harris, Dan, 1984

Women's Track

Wells, Sumetia, 1981–82
Hanna, Colleen, 1982
Bullocks, Denise, 1982

Kansas State University
Manhattan, Kansas 66506

All Big-Eight Conference

Men's Track

Switzer, Sr., Veryl, 1952
McGill, Ray, 1970
Alexander, Dale, 1974
Williams, Dean, 1974
Lee, Michael, 1974
Roland, Vance, 1974–75
Parrette, Vince, 1980
Switzer, Jr., Veryl, 1982

Women's Track

Hancock, Freda, 1978
Trent, Wanda, 1981
Graves, Rita, 1983
Suggs, Pinkie, 1984

All American

Switzer, Jr., Veryl, 1982–83

Women's Track

Graves, Rita, 1983–84
Suggs, Pinkie, 1984

University of Kansas
Lawrence, Kansas 66045

Coaches of Varsity Teams

Coffey, Carla (Assistant), 1980–88

All-American

Shelby, Ernest, LJ, 220YH 1958–59
Tidwell, Charles, 100YD, 200Y H 1958–59
Ard, Gary, LJ 1967
Lewis, Ed, 440YRT 1974
Edwards, Emmett, 440YRT 1974
Wiley, Clifford[1], 100M, 200M, MRT 1975–78
Newell, Kevin, 400MRT 1977–78
Blutcher, David, 400MRT 1978–80
Whitaker, Stan, MRT 1978–79
Mickens, Lester, 1,600MRT 1980
Hogan, Deon, 1,600MRT 1980

NCAA Champions

Shelby, Ernest, OD, LJ 1958–59
Tidwell, Charles, OD, 100MD, 220MD, 1958–60
Ard, Gary, OD, LJ, 1967
Jessie, Ron, ID, LJ, 1969
Ricks, Michael, ID, 600YD, 1980

University of Kansas Hall of Fame

Newell, Kevin
Wiley, Clifford
Edwards, Emmett
Tidwell, Charles
Shelby, Ernest
Ard, Gary
Jessie, Ron
Ricks, Michael

[1] Wiley, Clifford—member of the 1980 United States Olympic Track and Field Team

SOUTHERN CONFERENCE

1. Furman University
2. Marshall University
3. Appalachian State University
4. Davidson College
5. University of Tennessee-Chattanooga
6. East Tennessee State University

NORTH ATLANTIC CONFERENCE

1. Boston University
2. University of Hartford
3. Northeastern University

4. University of Delaware
5. University of Vermont
6. University of Maine

Boston University
Boston, Massachusetts 02215

Boston University's Hall of Fame

Thomas, John[1]
Bruce, Dr. Bernard

[1] Thomas, John—member of the 1960 and 1964 United States Olympic Track and Field Team

Northeastern University
Boston, Massachusetts 02115

All Greater Boston Conference

Little, William,[1] 1960–62
Cater, William,[2] 1964
Allen, Arthur, 1985

[1] Little, William—1960 Indoor 45-Yard High and Low Hurdles; 1961 Indoor 45-Yard High and Low Hurdles; 1962 Indoor 45-Yard Low Hurdles Champion
[2] Cater, William—1964 45-Yard Dash Champion; 1964 440-Yard Dash Champion

University of Delaware
Newark, Delaware 19716

Other Outstanding Athletes

Brown, Michael, 50YD
Gordy, Frank, TJ, 600YD
Gregory, Ted, SPT
Ingram, Michael, LJ
Price, Calvin, 200MD
Ramsey, Guy, HJ
Luck, Ken, LJ
Thompkins, Nathaniel, WT
Madric, James, TJ, HH
Johnson, Anthony, HH
Miller, Dan, WT, SP
Weston, James, LJ

University of Vermont
Burlington, Vermont 05405

All Yankee Conference

Howard, William C.,[1] 1951

[1] Howard, William C.—1990 New England Indoor 50-Yard Dash Champion

Division II Colleges

1. California State University, Los Angeles
2. California Polytechnic State University
3. Chicago State University
4. Texas A&I University
5. University of Puget Sound

6. Philadelphia College of Textiles and Sciences
7. University of Tennessee, Martin
8. City College of New York
9. Wesleyan University
10. Seattle University

California State University, Los Angeles
Los Angeles, California 90032

Coaches of Varsity Teams

Coleman, Leon (Head Acting), 1983

Cross Country

Bryant, Rosalyn (Head), 1981

All-American Division II

Men's Track

Lewis, Tony, LJ 1976
Adams, Keith, PV 1977
Hart, Chester, HH 1977–78
Turner, Sam, 400MH 1977–78, 1980
Peete, Gerald, 400M 1978

Robinson, Craig, PV 1978
Greene, Anthony, HH, IH 1979
Hopper, Clarence, IH 1980–81
Booker, Angelo, HH 1981
Gray, Byron, TJ 1982
Lister, Tom, SP 1982
Holmes, Gregg, 100M, 200M 1982–83
Williams, Eric, 200M 1983

Women's Track

Scott, Jarvis, AIAW 1973
Bryant, Rosalyn, AIAW 100M, 200M, 400M 1976–78
Rich, Yolanda, AIAW 400M 1979–80
Williams, Diane, NCAAI, 100M, 200M 1982–83
Howard, Denean, NCAAI, 400M 1983
Howard, Sherri, NCAAI, 100M, 200M 1984
Dabney, Sharon, NCAAI, 400M 1985

California State University's Hall of Fame

Bryant, Rosalyn

California Polytechnic State University
San Luis Obispo, California 93407

All-American

Turner, Cecil,[1] 100M, LJ, 1967–68
Brown, Reynaldo,[2] HJ, 1971–73
Edwards, Clancy,[3] 100M, 200M, 1974–75
Williams, Bart,[4] 400MH, 1978–79

[1] Turner, Cecil—Division II All-American
[2] Brown, Reynaldo—Division II All-American
[3] Edwards, Clancy—Division II All-American
[4] Williams, Bart—Division II All-American

Chicago State University
Chicago, Illinois 60628

Coaches of Varsity Teams

Davis, Sudie, 1977–90
Harris, Veronica, 1981–90

All-American

Curtis, Josephy, NAIA, 1978–79
Horton, Delwyn, NAIA, 1978–79

Texas A & I University
Kingsville, Texas 78363

Outstanding Athletes

Green, Darrell, 100MD, 200MD, 400MD
Gay, Stefan, 800MR
Sweeney, Bryan, 100MH
Martin, Demetrius, member 400MRT
Green, Darrel, member 400MRT

Texas A & I University's Hall of Fame

Haynes, Earnest

University of Puget Sound
Tacoma, Washington 98416

Coaches of Varsity Teams

Peyton, Joe, 1968–Present

All-American NAIA

Peyton, Joe—LJ, 1964

Wesleyan University
Middletown, Connecticut 06457

Outstanding Athletes

Logan, John
Johnson, James
Linder, Michael
Harris, Darrick
Cornwall, Milton
Robinson, Kevin
Smith, Al

Women's Track

Dillon, Neyga

CENTRAL INTERCOLLEGIATE ATHLETIC ASSOCIATION

1. Virginia State University
2. Norfolk State University
3. Virginia Union University
4. Fayetteville State University
5. Hampton University
6. Livingstone College
7. Johnson C. Smith University
8. Elizabeth City State University
9. Winston-Salem State University
10. Shaw University
11. St. Augustine's College
12. St. Paul's College
13. North Carolina Central University
14. Bowie State University

Hampton University
Hampton, Virginia 23668

Coaches of Varsity Teams

Women's Track

Sweat, Laverne, 1978–93

All-American

Richardson, Paul, NAIA (HH) 1976
Watts, William, NAIA (TJ) 1976
Powell, Whitney, NAIA (MR) 1979
Ruffin, Michael, NAIA (MR) 1979
Williams, Willie, NAIA (MR) 1979
West, Richard, NAIA (MR) 1979
Dixon, David, NCAA (HH) (ID) 1981
Brown, Robert, NAIA 440M (ID), 400M (OD)
Symonette, Ed, NAIA, (MR) (ID) 1982
Brown, Robert, NAIA (MR) (ID) 1982
Johnson, Freddie, NAIA (ID) 1982
Turner, Doug, NAIA (MR) (ID) 1982
Johnson, Freddie, NAIA 60YD (ID) 1982
Marshall, Livingstone, 800M (OD) NAIA 1983
Skinner, Darryl, 100M, NAIA 1983
Delk, Lee Roy, 4x100R, NAIA 1983
Brown, Robert, 4x100R, NAIA 1983
Dannelly, Charles, 4x100R, NAIA 1983
Skinner, Darryl, 4x100R, NAIA 1983
Delk, Lee Roy, 200M, NAIA 1983
Fisher, Kenneth, 800M, NAIA 1983
Mason, Mark, Discus, NAIA 1983

Livingstone College
Salisbury, North Carolina 28144

Coaches of Varsity Teams

Mitchell, Edward L., 1957–58
Brown, Arthur L., 1959–60
Cox, Charles R., 1960–64
Marshall, J.D., 1964–65, 1967–68
Seales, Roger, 1968–70
Ponder, Fred, 1970–73
Holman, Baxter D., 1973–78
Littlejohn, Andrew, 1978–79
Rose, Mel, 1980

North Carolina Central University
Durham, North Carolina 27707

Coaches of Varsity Teams

Walker, Dr. Leroy T., 1946–73
Jermundson, Aaron, 1973–75
Harvey, Robert, 1975–77
Lipscomb, George, 1977–81
Falcuma, McDougald Mark Adams, 1981–82
McDonald, Larry, 1982

Reference Section

MID-EASTERN ATHLETIC CONFERENCE

1. Morgan State University
2. Delaware State College
3. South Carolina State College
4. University of Maryland, Eastern Shore
5. Florida A&M University

6. North Carolina A&T State University
7. Howard University
8. Coppin State University
9. Bethune-Cookman College

Morgan State University
Baltimore, Maryland 21239

All-American

Rhoden, George, 1952
Bragg, Arthur "Art," 1953
Culbreath, Joshua "Josh," 1955
Lee, Nichols "Nick," 1966

Morgan State University's
Athletic Hall of Fame

Ross, Wellington "Duckie"
Couch, Flan "Butte"
Barksdale, A. Robert "Barky Roll"
Bragg, Arthur "Art"
Brown, William "Bill"
Ellis, Nochols "Nick"
Labeach, Samuel "Speedy"
Rhoden, George V.
Tyler, Robert "Bo"
Culbreath, Joshua "Josh"
Thompson, Lancelot "L.C."
Lee, Nichols "Nick"
Martin, Lee
Dennis, George Robert
Rogers, James "Jimmy"
Bethea, John David
Brown, Kelsey Thurlow
Wade, Herman "Bitsey"
Waters, Edward "Dickey"
Gross, Harry Rudolph
Kake, Kenneth
Morgan, Howard Phipps
Winder, Paul Lewis
Labeach, Byron
Stanbury, Wardell

Delaware State College
Dover, Delaware 19901

Coaches of Varsity Teams

Franklin, Frederick, 1953–67
Watson, Harrison B., 1967–70
Burden, Joseph, 1970–93

Women's Track

Hackett, Marvin, 1973–80
Elliott, Scott, 1980–81
Tullis, Walter, 1981–82
Sowerby, Fred, 1983–90
Meekins, Ricky, 1990–93

Cross Country

Burden, Joseph, 1980–81
Burke, Raymond, 1982–83
Sowerby, Fred, 1983–84
Meekins, Ricky, 1992–93

All-American (Black College)

Morris, Brad,[1] 1975
Tullis, Walter,[2] 1977
White, Gregory,[3] 1977
Howell, Emory,[4] 1977–79

Women's Track

Collins, Michelle, 1984
Dortch, Lorraine, 1984
Hunter, Sophia, 1984–85

[1] Morris, Brad—NCAA All-American
[2] Tullis, Walter—NAIA All-American
[3] White, Gregory—NAIA All-American
[4] Howell, Emory—NAIA All-American

University of Maryland, Eastern Shore
Princess Anne, Maryland 21853

Coaches of Varsity Teams

McCain, Vernon "Skip," 1949–56
Watson, Pop, 1956–58
Ross, Wilbur, 1958–60
Anderson, Clifton "Cappy," 1960–79
Brown, Robert, 1979–80
Sowerby, Fred, 1980–83
Daley, Ian, 1983–90
Hodge, Neville, 1990–93

All Central Intercollegiate Athletic Association

Rogers, Russ,[1] 1961–63
Mays, Charles, 1961–63
Santio, Al, 1962
Cayenne, Benedict
Skinner, Ed, 1962
Gilbert, Elius, 1963
Jackson, Raymond, 1963
Jones, Cliff, 1963
Bush, Edward, 1963
Carmen, Jon, 1963
Rogers, Earl, 1963–65

All Mid-Eastern Athletic Conference

Daly, Ian, 1982
Thomas, Greg, 1982
Meekins, Rickey,[2] 1982–83
Bell, Robert,[3] 1982–83
Addison, David,[4] 1982–84
Harrigan, Annette, 1983–84
Anderson, Natalie,[5] 1983–85
Pierce, Kimberly, 1983–85
Tyer, Angela, 1983–85

[1] Rogers, Russ—member of the 1964 Olympic Track and Field Team
[2] Meekins, Rickey—Cross Country Champion; 1500 Outdoor Champion
[3] Bell, Robert—Cross Country
[4] Addison, David—Cross Country
[5] Anderson, Natalie—Cross Country; Most Outstanding Female Performer at MEAC Outdoor Track Championship

Florida A&M University
Tallahassee, Florida 32207

Coaches of Varsity Teams

Griffin, Peter, 1955–61

Hill, Richard, 1961–64
Gibson, Ken, 1964–66
Lang, Bobby, 1966–93

North Carolina
A&T State University
Greensboro, North Carolina 27411

Coaches of Varsity Teams

Thompson, Roy, 1990–93

Howard University
Washington, D.C. 20059

Coaches of Varsity Teams

Chambers, Ted, 1945–49
Moultrie, William, 1973–93

All-American

Men's Track

Corley, Hayward, MR, 1975
White, Gosnell, MR 1975–77
Sojourner, Reginald, MR, 1,600MR, 1975, 1977–78
Massey, Richard, MR, 400M, 1,600MR, 1975–78
Jones, Zachary, MR, 1,600MR, 1977–78
Archie, Michael, MR, 1,600MR, 1977–78
Bridges, Oliver, MR, 400M, 1,600MR, 1981–83
Charleton, David, MR, 1,600MR, 1981–83
Oliver, Bernard, MR, 1981–82
Sims, Ed, MR, 1981–82
Wilson, Kenneth, 1,600MR, 1983
Louis, Richard, 1,600MR, 500M, 1983, 1985
Skerritt, Anton, 500M, 1985

Women's Track

Wilson, Dorothy, 1,600MR, 1982
Brooks, Kimberly, 1,600MR, 1982
Murphy, Debra, 1,600MR, 1982
Charles, Ruberta, 1,600MR, 1982, 1984
Pough, Michele, 1,600MR, 1984
Brooks, Kathy, 1,600MR, 1984
Allen, Teresa, LJ, 1985

Coppin State College
Baltimore, Maryland 21216

Coaches of Varsity Teams

Men's and Women's Cross Country
Meyers, Dr. John, 1967–69
Jackson, Fletcher, 1969–74
Smith, Lewis, 1974–78
Merritt, Michael, 1983–84
Brown, Larry, 1984–Present

Track
Brown, Larry, 1984–90
Webster, Donald, 1990–93

Bethune-Cookman College
Daytona Beach, Florida 32015

Coaches of Varsity Teams
Culver, Terence, 1990–93

SOUTHWESTERN ATHLETIC CONFERENCE

1. Alcorn State University
2. Grambling State University
3. Prairie View A&M University
4. Southern University

5. Jackson State University
6. Texas Southern University
7. Mississippi Valley State University
8. Alabama State University

Jackson State University
Jackson, Mississippi 39217

Coaches of Varsity Teams

Norris, Edward P., 1946–50
Ellis, T.B., 1950–53
Merritt, John, 1953–54
Blackburn, Benjamin, 1954–64
Lattimore, Henry, 1964–69
Epps, Martin, 1968–90

Women's Track and Field
Epps, Martin, 1969–90

Texas Southern University
Houston, Texas 77004

Coaches of Varsity Teams

Retting, E.V., 1946–48
Wright, Stanley V., 1951–67
Paul, Clifford, 1968–69
Bethany, David, 1970–93

Southwestern Athletic Conference Hall of Fame

Inductees (May 1992)

Southern University • Rodney Milburn, Track

BIG TEN CONFERENCE

1. Purdue University
2. University of Wisconsin
3. Northwestern University
4. Indiana University
5. Ohio State University
6. Iowa University

7. University of Illinois at Urbana-Champaign
8. University of Minnesota
9. Michigan State University
10. University of Michigan
11. Pennsylvania State University

Purdue University
West Lafayette, Indiana 47097

Coaches of Varsity Teams

Women's Track
Grissom, Jo Ann, 1975–76

All Big Ten Conference

Men's Track
Gay, Stan, 1968–69
Fulton, Mel, 1969
Laing, Derek, 1978
Cammack, Ken, 1978–80, 1980–82
McNair, Alvin, 1983–84

Women's Track
Payne, Peach, 1979
Perry, Sybil, 1982–85
Netterville, Yvonne, 1983–85

All-American

Men's Track
Adams, Nate, 1963
Gay, Stan, 1968
Burton, Larry, 1974
Cammack, Ken, 1980
McNair, Alvin, 1983

Women's Track
Payne, Peach, 1979
Russell, Lorna, 1982
Perry, Sybil, 1982
Netterville, Yvonne, 1984

University of Wisconsin
Madison, Wisconsin 53711

Coaches of Varsity Teams

Men's Track
Dockery, Al (Assistant), 1974–90

Women's Track
Henderson, Douglas (Assistant), 1983–90

Big-Ten Champions

Nixon, Jesse, OD 440YD, 1963
Nixon, Jesse, ID 600YD, 1959
Pitts, Terry, ID 600YD, 1962
Higginbottom, Elzie, ID OMR, 1962
Howard, Larry, ID 70Y HH, 1962
Stalling, Reginald, ID OMR, 1966
Arrington, Ray, ID 880YR, 1967–69
Stalling, Reginald, ID OMR, 1966
Butler, Michael, ID 70Y HH, 1967–69
Johnson, Greg, ID 70Y LH, 1970
Johnson, Lawrence, ID 60YD, 1976
Higginbottom, Elzie, OD 440YD, 1963
Jackson, Aquine, OD 100YD, 1967
Arrington, Ray, OD MR, 1,500M, 880YR, 1967–69
Butler, Michael, OD 100YD, OD 120Y HH, 1968–69
Bond, Michael, OD TJ, 1968–69
Hewlett, Dial, OD OMR, 1969
Floyd, Larry, OD OMR, 1969
Johnson, Greg, OD LJ, 1970
Johnson, Lawrence, OD 100MD, 200MD, OMR, 1976–77
Hand, Rich, OD 100M HH, 1977
Dixon, Leroy, OD 400MD, 1983
Toon, Al, ID TJ, 1984

Northwestern University
Evanston, Illinois 60201

Coaches of Varsity Teams

Women's Track and Cross Country
Todd, Dee, 1981–85

Northwestern University's Hall of Fame
Golliday, James

Indiana University
Bloomington, Indiana 47405

All-American

Harris, Archie—Discus Throw

Indiana University's Hall of Fame
Bell, Greg[1]
Campbell, Milt[2]

[1] Bell, Greg—member of the 1956 United States Olympic Track and Field Team
[2] Campbell, Milt—member of the 1952 and 1956 United States Olympic Track and Field Team

Ohio State University
Columbus, Ohio 43210-1166

Coaches of Varsity Teams

Women's Track and Field
Rallins, Mamie (Head), 1977–93

All-American
Whitfield, Mal,[1] 1948–49

Women's Track
Hightower, Stephanie,[2] 1978–80

Ohio State University's Hall of Fame
Owens, Jesse
Albritton, David
Whitfield, Malvin

[1] Whitfield, Mal—member of the 1948 United States Olympic Track and Field Team; 800 meters NCAA champion; 1948 and 1949, 1954 Sullivan Award recipient (given to the nation's top amateur athlete).
[2] Hightower, Stephanie—member of the 1980 United States Olympic Track and Field Team

Iowa University
Iowa City, Iowa 52242

Coaches of Varsity Teams

Men's Track and Cross Country
Wheeler, Ted (Head), 1978

University of Illinois at Urbana-Champaign
Champaign, Illinois 61820

All Big-Ten Conference

Women's Track and Field
Washington, Bev, HJ, 1976–78
Conda, Roland, 400M, 1982–83
Grier, Gretchen, 800MR, 600YD, 1982–83
Dunlap, Kim, OD 400MR, 1983
Bass, Rachel, OD 400MR, 1983

All-American

Women's Track and Field
Ward, Cheryl, 3,200MR, 1982
Griet, Gretchen, 800MR, 3,200MR, 1982
Conda, Rolanda, 800MR, 1982

Michigan State University
East Lansing, Michigan 48824

Coaches of Varsity Teams

Women's Track and Field
Jackson, Nell (Head), 1973–77, 1979–81

Women's Track and Field, Cross Country
Dennis, Karen (Head), 1982

ATLANTIC COAST CONFERENCE

1. University of North Carolina, Chapel Hill
2. University of Virginia
3. Wake Forest University
4. University of Maryland, College Park
5. Georgia Institute of Technology

6. Duke University
7. Clemson University
8. North Carolina State University
9. Florida State University

University of Maryland
College Park, Maryland 20740

All-American

Nehemiah, Renaldo—110M, 1979–80

Georgia Institute of Technology
Atlanta, Georgia 30332

Coaches of Varsity Teams

Women's Track and Cross Country
Todd, Dee (Head), 1985–93

All Atlantic Coast Conference

Horton, Bob, 1979
Larkin, Jeff, 1982
Stiles, Raymond, 1982
Armour, Michael, 1983–85

Bernard, Carlyle, 1983–85
Purvis, James, 1985
Morris, Dirk, 1985

All-American

Lowe, Larry, 1977–78
Hughes, Donald, 1978
Wade, Greg, 1978–79
Larkin, Jeff, 1979–80
Stiles, Raymond, 1982
Alexander, Phil, 1982
Bernard, Carlyle, 1983
Armour, Michael, 1983–84
McKay, Antonio, 1984–85
Morris, Dirk, 1985
Stanley, James, 1985

PAC-TEN CONFERENCE

1. Stanford University
2. University of Washington
3. University of Southern California
4. University of California, Los Angeles
5. University of Arizona

6. Arizona State University
7. University of California, Berkeley
8. University of Oregon
9. Oregon State University
10. Washington State University

Stanford University
Stanford, California 94305

Coaches of Varsity Teams
Johnson, Brooks (Head),[1] 1978–90

All-American

Stoecker, Robert, 1965–66
Frische, Eric[1], 1965

Rubin, Dale,[2] 1965
McIntyre, Robert,[3] 1965
Questad, Larry,[4] 1965

Women's Track
Jacoba, Regina, 1500M, 1983–84

[1] Frische, Eric—member of the 440-Yard Relay Team
[2] Rubin, Dale—member of the 440-Yard Relay Team
[3] McIntyre, Robert—member of the 440-Yard Relay Team
[4] Questad, Larry—member of the 440-Yard Relay Team

University of Washington
Seattle, Washington 98105

All Pacific-Eight or Pacific-Ten Conference

Gaines, Spider,[1] 1976

Other Outstanding Athletes

Gayton, Gary[2]
Franco, Pablo[3]

[1] Gaines, Spider—High Hurdles Champion, 1976
[2] Gayton, Gary—Two-Mile Run; 800 Meters
[3] Franco, Pablo—100-Meter and Mile Relay

University of Southern California
Los Angeles, California 90089-0602

Coaches of Varsity Teams

Davis, Leo

NCAA Champions

McCullough, Earl, HH, 1967–68
Miller, Lennox, 100MD, 1968
Edwards, Clancy, 100MD, 1978
Mullins, William, 400MD, 1978
Williams, Kevin, S R, 1978
Sanford, James, 1979

Other Outstanding Athletes

Cook, Darwin

University of California, Los Angeles
Los Angeles, California 90024

All Pacific Coast and All Pacific-Ten Conference

Alexander, Kermit, TJ, 1962
Jackson, Norman, 440 YRT, 1966
Copeland, Ron, HH, 1967
Smith, John, 440YD, 1970
Collett, Wayne, 440YD, 1971
Robinson, Reginald, 440YRT, 1971
Echols, Reginald, 440YRT, 1971
Edmonson, Warren, 440YRT, 1971
Collett, Wayne, 440YRT, 1971
Butts, James, TJ, 1972

Rich, Charles, HH, 1972
Gaddis, Ron, MR, 1972
Echols, Reginald, MR, 1972
Brown, Ben, MR, 1972
Tiff, Milan, TJ, 1973
Jackson, Clim, HH, 1975
Owens, James, HH, 1977
Thompson, Donn, MR, 1977
Myles, Bennie, MR, 1977
Banks, Willie, TJ, 1978
Brown, Eric, 100M, 1981–82
Davis, Del, HJ, 1982

NCAA Champions

Luvalle, James,[1] 440YD, 1935
Lacefield, William, LJ, 1938
Robinson, Jackie, LJ, 1940
Brown, George,[2] LJ, 1951–52
Johnson, Jim, HH, 1960
Alexander, Kermit, TJ, 1962
Copeland, Ron, HH, 1966
Smith, John, MRT, 440YD, 1969–71
Collett, Wayne, MRT, 1969–71
Echols, Reginald, MRT, 1971–72
Edmonson, Warren, MRT, 100M, 1971–72
Butts, James, TJ, 1972
Gaddis, Ron, 1972–73
Peppers, Gordon, MRT, 1973
Tiff, Milan, TJ, 1973
Walters, Jerome, MRT, 1974
Herndon, Jerry, LJ, 1974
Owens, James, HH, 1977
Foster, Greg, HH, 1978–80
Phillips, Andre, 1981
Davis, Del, HJ, 1982

National TAC Champions

Johnson, Rafer,[3] 1956–58, 1960
Smith, John, 440YD, 1970–71
Owens, James, HH, 1977
Tiff, Milan, TJ, 1977
Butts, James, TJ, 1978
Banks, Willie,[4] 1980–81, 1983
Foster, Greg,[5] HH, 1981–83

All-American

Women's Track

White, Sharon, 1975
Butler, Gayle, 1975
Roberson, Debra, 1976–77
Ashford, Evelyn,[6] 1976–78
Gourdine, Lisa, 1978
Warner, Cynthia, 1980
Ward, Andrea, 1980
Law, Kim, 1980
Fowler, Oralee, 1980
Cumbess, Cindy, 1980–81
Howard, Sherri, 1981
Emerson, Arlise, 1980–82
Jerald, Missy, 1981–82
Bolden, Jeannette,[7] 1981–83
Griffith, Florence,[8] 1982–83
Alston, Tonya, 1984
Joyner, Jackie,[9] 1984

Other Outstanding Athletes

Bradley, Thomas

[1] Luvalle, James—member of the 1936 United States Olympic Track and Field Team
[2] Brown, George—member of the 1952 United States Olympic Track and Field Team
[3] Johnson, Rafer—Decathlon; member of the 1956 and 1960 United States Olympic Track and Field Teams
[4] Banks, Willie—member of the 1984 United States Olympic Track and Field Team
[5] Foster, Greg—member of the 1984 United States Olympic Track and Field Team
[6] Ashford, Evelyn—member of the 1984 United States Olympic Track and Field Team
[7] Bolden, Jeanette—member of the 1984 United States Olympic Track and Field Team
[8] Griffith, Florence—member of the 1984 United States Olympic Track and Field Team
[9] Joyner, Jackie—member of the 1984 United States Olympic Track and Field Team

University of Arizona
Tucson, Arizona 85721

Coaches of Varsity Teams

Williams, Willie[1] (Head), 1970–82

[1] Williams, Willie—1972 and 1973 NCAA District Seven Coach of the Year; first black head track coach at a major university

University of California, Berkeley
Berkeley, California 97420

Coaches of Varsity Teams

Craig, Charles (Assistant), 1970
Hunt, Ervin J. (Head), 1972–90

All Pacific-Ten or Pacific-Eight Conference

Men's Track and Field

White, Wille, 100Y, 1960
Strickland, Howard, 1974
Robinson, James, 800M, 1975
Cowling, Larry, 110MH, 1981
Bates, Paul, TJ, 1981
Robinson, Leonard, 400MH, 1983

Women's Track

Culbaert, Connie, 1983
Arnold, Jean, 1984
Cole, Gina, 1984
Wite, Kim, 1984

Other Outstanding Athletes

Williams, Archie[1]
Hart, Ed[2]

[1] Williams, Archie—member of the 1936 United States Olympic Track and Field Team
[2] Hart, Ed—member of the 1972 United States Olympic Track and Field Team

University of Oregon
Eugene, Oregon 97403

All Pacific Coast, All Pacific-Eight, or All Pacific-Ten Conference

Lewis, Woodley, NDC, BJ, 1948–50
Barnes, Emery, NDC, HJ, 1952
Davis, Otis, NDC, 220YD, 1958
Moore, Bouncey, LJ, 1970
Mack, David, 800M, 1980
Walcott, George, 200MC, 1983

All-American

Cook, Roscoe,[1] 1959
Davis, Otis,[2] 1960
Renfro, Mel, 1962

Buford, Vincent, S., 1970
Moore, Bouncy, LJ, 1970
Heavy, Al, 1970–72
Vance, Weldon, 1971
Harris, Ivory, HH, 1971–72
Mack, Davis, 800M, 1980–81

Women's Track
Adams, Debbie,[3] 1979
Batiste, Melanie,[4] 1979–81
Massey, Rhonda,[5] 1979–80
Beasley, Queena,[6] 1983

[1] Cook, Roscoe—Collegiate Champion, 100-Yard Dash
[2] Davis, Otis—400 Meters; member of the 1960 United States Olympic Track
   and Field Team
[3] Adams, Debbie—AIAW All-American Mile Relay
[4] Batiste, Melanie—AIAW All-American Mile Relay
[5] Massey, Rhonda—AIAW All-American Mile Relay
[6] Beasley, Queena—NCAA All-American; Shot Put

Oregon State University
Corvallis, Oregon 97331

Coaches of Varsity Teams
Simmons, Steven (Head), 1976–79

All-American
Turner, Willie, 220 YD 1970

Washington State University
Pullman, Washington 99164-1610

Washington State University's Hall of Fame
Foster, Wes

Other Outstanding Athletes
Foster, Wes
Richardson, Clint
Kimble, Ray
Brewster, James
Whitlock, Chris
Gordon, Lee

IVY LEAGUE CONFERENCE

1. Harvard University
2. Princeton University
3. Dartmouth College
4. Cornell University
5. Columbia University
6. Yale University
7. University of Pennsylvania
8. Brown University

Harvard University
Cambridge, Massachusetts 02138

Harvard University's Hall of Fame

Cross Country
Wharton, Richard G.[1]

[1] Wharton, Richard G.—earned varsity letters in cross country, 1954–56

Princeton University
Princeton, New Jersey 08544

All Ivy League

Men's Track
Stevenson, Herman, 1970

Women's Track
Newsam, Mary Elizabeth

Dartmouth College
Hanover, New Hampshire 03755

All Ivy League

Norman, Ken, 600DR 1975–76
Nichols, Rich, 600DR 1976

Outdoor Track

Norman, Ken, 440YR, 400M 1975–76
O'Neal, Shawn, 1,500M 1982

All-American

Norman, Ken, 1975–76
Nichols, Rich, 1975–76
Worrell, Carl, 1976
Coburn, Robert, 1978

Cornell University
Ithaca, New York 14851

Women's Track and Cross Country
Evans, Renee (Head), 1978–82

All-American

Men's Track
Hall, Neal, 200M, 1977

Women's Track
Roach, Palemetisa, 1975

Cornell University's Hall of Fame
Leonard, Jim[1]

[1] Leonard, Jim—1972, 1974–75 Heptagonal Outdoor Triple Jump Champion

Columbia University—Barnard College
New York, New York 10027

All-American

Johnson, Ben, 1936
Allen, Charles, 1977

Other Outstanding Athletes

Armstrong, Paul

Yale University
New Haven, Connecticut 06250

Coaches of Varsity Teams

Calhoun, Lee (Head), 1975–80

All Ivy League

Men's Track

Jones, Paul, 1968
Hill, Calvin,[1] 1969
Martin, Don,[2] 1971
Osborne, Martin,[3] 1980
Profit, Eugene,[4] 1983
Miller, Larry,[5] 1984
Wiggins, Douglas,[6] 1985

Women's Track

Melton, Patricia,[7] 1981–82
Forbes, Moya,[8] 1982

All-American

Women's Track

Melton, Patricia, 400MH, 1982

Other Outstanding Athletes

Motley, Wendell[9]

[1] Hill, Calvin—IC4A Long Jump Champion, Heptagonal Long and Triple Jump Champion
[2] Martin, Don—IC4A and Heptagonal Dash Champion
[3] Osborne, Martin—Steeplechase
[4] Profit, Eugene—Heptagonal Long Jump Champion
[5] Miller, Larry—Heptagonal Long Jump Champion
[6] Wiggins, Douglas—Heptagonal Long Jump Champion
[7] Melton, Patricia—400-Meter Hurdles
[8] Forbes, Moya—Indoor Heptagonal 200-Meter Champion
[9] Motley, Wendell—member of the 1964 United States Olympic Track and Field Team

University of Pennsylvania
Philadelphia, Pennsylvania 19104

Other Outstanding Athletes

Track and Cross Country
Cochran-Fikes, Denis Elton[1]

[1] Cochran-Fikes, Denis Elton—captain of the team, 1974

SOUTHWEST CONFERENCE

1. Texas Christian University
2. Rice University
3. Baylor University
4. Texas Tech University

5. Texas A&M University
6. Southern Methodist University
7. University of Texas, Austin
8. University of Houston, University Park

Texas Christian University
Fort Worth, Texas 76129

All-American

Williams, Lee, 1974
Collins, William, 1974–75
Delaney, Phillip, 1974–75
McKinney, Andrew "Sam," 1975
Norris, Glen, 1975–76
Milton, Michael, 1976
Boone, Cleo, 1976
Thomas, Jerry, 1976
Thomas, Jerry, 1976
Epps, Phillip, 1982–83
Walker, David, 1983
Ingraham, Allen, 1983
Richard, James, 1983
Burnett, Keith, 1983–84
Cannon, Michael, 1984

Baylor University
Waco, Texas 76706

All-American

Carter, Michael, 1975–76
Duncan, Davey, 1976
Reed, Scooter, 1976
Fisher, Michael, 1978
Clarke, Chris, 1978–80
Vaughn, Vance, 1980
Jefferson, Zeke, 1980–81
Davis, Bruce, 1981
McCullar, Arthur, 1981
Caldwell, Willie, 1982

Texas Tech University
Lubbock, Texas 79409

All-American

Mays, James, 800M, 1981
Selmon, Thomas, 1981
Poyser, Delroy, 1983–84

Texas A&M University
College Station, Texas 77843-1228

Harvey, Edgar, 1968
McElroy, Hugh, 1968
Mills, Curtis, 1970
Mills, Marvin, 1970
Blackmon, Willie, 1970–71
Taylor, Marvin, 1975–76
Jones, Scottie, 1975–76
Brooks, Ray, 1978
Figgs, Kent, 1978
Dickey, Curtis, 1978–80
Willis, Steven, 1979–80
Kerr, Leslie, 1979–81
Pittman, Vernon, 1979–82
Jamerson, Reginald, 1980
Figgs, Karl, 1980
Washington, James, 1980–82
Gillespie, Michael, 1981–82
Austin, Darrell, 1982
Jones, Don, 1982
Tolson, Tony, 1982

All-American

Mills, Curtis, 1970
Dickey, Curtis, 1979–80
Henderson, Chapelle, 1983

Southern Methodist University
Dallas, Texas 75275

All-American

Shaw, Rufus, 220M, 440YR, 1973–74
Pouncy, Joe, 220M, 440YR, 1973–74
Pouncy, Eugene, 100M, 440YR, 1973–74
Carter, Michael,[1] 1980

[1] Carter, Michael—shot put; member of the 1984 United States Olympic Track and Field Team

University of Texas at Austin
Austin, Texas 78713-7389

Women's Track

Turner, Terry, MR, 440M, 1983–84
Walker, Florence, TMR, 1,600MR, 1983–84

All-American

Women's Track

Coleman, Robbin, 600YR, MR, 1982
Sherfield, Donna, MR, 400MR, 1982
Denny, Hollie, 400MR, 1982
Walker, Florence, MR, 1982
Turner, Terry, TJ, 1984
Johnson, Robyne, TJ, 1984

[1] Jones, John "Lam"—member of the 1976 United States Olympic Track and Field Team

University of Houston, University Park,
Houston, Texas 77004

All-American

Men's Track

Edwards, Rich, 1979
Lewis, Carl,[1] 1980–81
Clark, Cletus, 1981
Floyd, Stanley, 1982
Ketchum, Anthony, 1982
McNeil, Mark, 1982
Berry, Andre, 1982
Young, Charles, 1982
Baptiste, Kirk, 1983
Criddle, Byron, 1983

Women's Track

Clary, Rachel, 1981
Lavallias, Pat, 1982
Jefferson, Darlene, 1982
Lewis, Carol, 1982
Sutton, Valarie, 1982
Mastin, Tara, 1983

[1] Lewis, Carl—member of the 1984 United States Olympic Track and Field Team

ATLANTIC-TEN CONFERENCE

1. West Virginia University
2. St. Bonaventure University
3. Temple University
4. Duquesne University
5. Rutgers University
6. University of Massachusetts
7. University of Rhode Island
8. St. Joseph's University
9. George Washington University

St. Bonaventure University
St. Bonaventure, New York 14778

Other Outstanding Athletes

Major, Charles[1]

[1] Major, Charles—National Indoor High Jump Champion

Temple University
Philadelphia, Pennsylvania 19122

Coaches of Varsity Teams

Alexander, Charles, (Head), 1977–90

Rutgers University
New Brunswick, New Jersey 08903

Coaches of Varsity Teams

Women's Track
Petway, Sandra (Head), 1973–80

Track
Williams, Robert (Assistant), 1969–74
McBryde, Ken (Assistant), 1980–84
Freeman, Ron (Assistant), 1981–82
Williams, David (Head), 1984

All-American

Grimes, Brian,[1] 1981
Belin, Ron,[2] 1981
Kirkland, Walter,[3] 1981

Women's Track
McCauley, Lori, 1984

[1] Grimes, Brian—member of the 1981 Indoor 880 Relay National Championship Team
[2] Belin, Ron—member of the 1981 Indoor 880 Relay National Championship Team
[3] Kirkland, Walter—member of the 1981 Indoor 880 Relay National Championship Team

University of Rhode Island
Kingston, Rhode Island 02881

All-American

Brown, Herman "Butch," 1982–83

INDEPENDENTS

1. Case Western Reserve University   2. University of Notre Dame

---

University of Notre Dame
Notre Dame, Indiana 46556

All-American

Lewis, Aubrey, 1958
Gregory, Ron, 1961
Hurd, William, 1969

SOUTHERN INTERCOLLEGIATE
ATHLETIC CONFERENCE*

1. Savannah State College   5. Clark College
2. Fort Valley State College   6. Morehouse College
3. Morris Brown College   7. Fisk University
4. Alabama A&M University

*The SIAC office did not provide information for the update of this edition.

Savannah State College
Savannah, Georgia 31404

Coaches of Varsity Teams
Wright, Theodore, 1949–56
Washington, Richard, 1956–75, 1985

Fort Valley State College
Fort Valley, Georgia 31030

Coaches of Varsity Teams
Craig, Richard, 1946–54
Lomax, Leon J., 1963–66

Mangrum, Leland, 1974–77
Rhodes, John, 1977–80
Jackson, Thomas, 1980–82
Turner, Glen, 1983–86

Women's Track
Love, Flossie, 1960–73
Marshall, Doris Lee, 1974–93

METRO CONFERENCE

1. University of Louisville
2. University of Southern Mississippi
3. Tulane University
4. Virginia Polytechnic Institute

University of Southern Mississippi
Hattiesburg, Mississippi 39406-3161

Coaches of Varsity Teams

Cross Country/Track
Bell, Marshall (Head), 1978–84

Other Outstanding Athletes

Cross Country
Young, Donnie

Virginia Polytechnic Institute
Blacksburg, Virginia 24061

Other Outstanding Athletes
Gaines, Jerry[1]

[1] Gaines, Jerry—the first black athlete to attend Virginia Tech Institute, 1967

GREAT MIDWEST CONFERENCE

1. University of Cincinnati
2. Memphis State University
3. University of Alabama, Birmingham
4. Marquette University
5. University of Saint Louis
6. DePaul University

METRO ATLANTIC CONFERENCE

1. Fordham University
2. La Salle University
3. St. Peter's College
4. College of the Holy Cross
5. Iona College
6. Manhattan College
7. Niagara University
8. Canisius College
9. Siena College

Fordham University
Bronx, New York 10458

Fordham University's Hall of Fame
Perry, Sam

BIG SKY CONFERENCE

1. Idaho State University
2. Northern Arizona University

3. Eastern Washington University

Idaho State University
Pocatello, Idaho 83209

All Rocky Mountain Conference

Malstrom, William, TJ 1964
Frazier, Len "Buddy," 220Y 1965
Bell, Ed, 220Y 1969
Lawson, Carl, 100Y, 220Y 1971–74

Northern Arizona University
Flagstaff, Arizona 86011

All-American

Cross Country
Chumley, Larry, 1984

OHIO VALLEY CONFERENCE

1. Eastern Kentucky University
2. Tennessee Technological University
3. Austin Peay State University
4. Middle Tennessee State University

5. Youngstown State University
6. Murray State University
7. Tennessee State University
8. Morehead State University

Tennessee Technological University
Cookeville, Tennessee 38505

Other Outstanding Athletes

Moore, Rodney

Middle Tennessee State University
Murfreesboro, Tennessee 37132

All-American

McClure, Barry, TJ 1972–73
Haynes, Tom,[1] TJ and LF 1975
Dupree, Rayfield,[2] TJ 1977
Artis, Greg,[3] LJ 1980–82
Lloyd, Eddie, TJ 1982
Meeks, Orestes, 1982
Johnson, Dwight, LJ 1984

[1] Haynes, Tom—member of the 1976 United States Olympic Track and Field Team
[2] Dupree, Rayfield—member of the 1976 United States Olympic Track and Field Team
[3] Artis, Greg—1981 Ohio Valley Conference Athlete of the Year

Tennessee State University
Nashville, Tennessee 37203

Coaches of Varsity Teams

Men's Track
Harris, Tom, 1945–55
Mack, Richard L., 1955–57
Kemp, Raymond, 1957–61
Stevens, Willie, 1961–67
Boyd, David, 1978–82
Foreman, Hezakiah, 1982–85

Women's Track
Harris, Tom, 1946–50
Kincaide, C. J., 1950–53
Temple, Edward S.,[1] 1953–93

All-American (Black College)
Boston, Ralph,[2] AAU Broad Jump, 1960–61

All-American
Patterson, Audrey, AAU, 200M Champion, 1948 (member of the 1948 United States Olympic Track and Field Team)

Reed, Emma, AAU, High Jump, 1948 (member of the 1948 United States Olympic Track and Field Team)

Patton, Jean, AAU, 200M, 1951

Faggs, Starr Mae, AAU, 100 Yard Dash, 1954–56 (member of the 1952 and 1956 United States Olympic Track and Field Team)

Daniels, Isabelle, AAU, 400M Relay Team, 1956–59 (member of the 1952 United States Olympic Track and Field Team)

Slater Jones, Barbara, AAU, 1958–59 (member of the 1960 United States Olympic Track and Field Team)

Wilburn, Margaret Matthews, AAU, Broad Jump, Sprints, 1957–59 (member of the 1956 United States Olympic Track and Field Team)

White, Willye B., AAU, Long Jump, 1960, 1964, 1968 and 1974, 1956–57 (member of the 1956, 1960, 1964, 1968, 1972 United States Olympic Track and Field Team)

Rudolph, Wilma, AAU, 100M Dash, Relay team, 1956–57, 1959, 1962 (member of the 1956 and 1960 United States Olympic Track and Field Team; 1960 Helms World Trophy recipient; 1961 James A. Sullivan Award recipient; 1960 Associated Press "Female Athlete of the Year" Award recipient)

Grissom, Joe Ann, AAU, Hurdles, Broad Jump, 1959–63 (member of the 1960 United States Olympic Track and Field Team)

Hudson, Martha, AAU, 100 Yard Dash, 1959 (member of the 1960 United States Olympic Track and Field Team)

Brown Reed, Vivian, AAU, 220 Yard Dash, 200 Meter Dash, 1961–62 (member of the 1964 United States Olympic Track and Field Team)

McGuire, Duvall, Edith, AAU, 100 and 200 Meter Dash, 1961, 1963, 1966 (member of the 1964 United States Olympic Track and Field Team)

Tyus Simberg, Wyomia, AAU, 100 Yard Dash, 100 Meter Dash, 1964 (member of the 1964 and 1968 United States Olympic Track and Field Team)

Montgomery, Eleanor, AAU, High Jump, 1966–69 (member of the 1968 United States Olympic Track and Field Team; 1969 Norma E. Seattle Award recipient)

Manning Jackson, Madeline, AAU, 400 Meter Dash, 800 Meters, 1968–72 (member of the 1968 United States Olympic Track and Field Team)

Watson, Martha, AAU, Long Jump, 1967–69 (member of the 1964, 1968, 1972 United States Olympic Track and Field Team)

Render, Mattilene, AAU, 60 Yard Dash, 100 Yard Dash, 1969–71

Davis Hicks, Iris, AAU, 100 Meter Dash, 1969–73

Cheesebourough, Chandra, 1979 (member of the 1984 United States Olympic Track and Field Team)

Tennessee State University's Hall of Fame

Coaches

Temple, Edward Stanley
Kemp, Ray

Men's Track

Boston, Ralph
Stevens, Willie
Moon, John

Women's Track

Patton, Jean
Faggs, Mae
Williams, Lucinda
Daniels, Isabelle
White, Willye B.
Hudson, Martha
Jones, Barbara
Rudolph, Wilma
McGuire, Edith
Tyvs, Wyomia
Watson, Martha
Manning, Madeline

[1] Temple, Edward S.—1960 and 1964 United States Olympic Women's Track and Field Coach; member of The United States Olympic Committee, 1960–80
[2] Boston, Ralph—member of the 1964 and 1968 United States Olympic Track and Field Team

INDEPENDENTS (BLACK COLLEGES)

1. University of the District of Columbia
2. Lincoln University (Pennsylvania)
3. Kentucky State University
4. Cheyney University of Pennsylvania
5. Bishop College

University of the District of Columbia
Washington, D.C. 20008

Coaches of Varsity Teams

Men's Track

Carr, Anthony, 1977
Stewart, James, 1978–82
Mullins, Stan, 1982–Present

Women's Track

Dixon, Adrian, 1977–79
Stanton, Harry, 1980–81
Mullins, Stan, 1982–Present

Cross Country

Dixon, Adrian, 1977–79

All-American

Men's Track

Brown, Anthony, ID and OD, 1985

Women's Track

Young, Elizabeth, 1979
Young, Yolene, 1985
Bushrod, Diane, 1985
Gooding, Marcelle, ID and OD, 1985

Lincoln University
Lincoln University, Pennsylvania 19352

All-American (Black College)

Parker, Alfonso, 1979
Williams, Robert, 1979
Hunt, Ron, 1979
Blanton, John, 1980
Bailey, Walter, 1980–81
Randolph, Michael, 1980–81
Hunt, William, 1981
Auston, Jeff, 1981–83

Youngblood, Van, 1981–83
Jones, Andre, 1982
Cunningham, Louis, 1982
Hammond, Robin, 1982
Fearon, Barry, 1983
Randolph, Cary, 1984

Kentucky State University
Frankfort, Kentucky 40601

Coaches of Varsity Teams

Gibson, Kenneth, 1967–69
Taylor, C. Randolph
Exum, William
Taylor, C. Randolph

All-American (NAIA)

Knox, Donald, 1964
Harris, Rudy, 1964
Ewing, Richard, 1964
Bradford, Mackey, 1965
Mullins, Stan, 1965
Kemp, James, 1967
Ray, Clarence, 1967
Wallace, Craig, 1968
Gary, Philip, 1968
Penn, James, 1969
Jordan, Steven, 1970–72
Pinkston, Allen, 1970–71
Garrett, Dick, 1971
Murphy, Ronald, 1971
Stallworth, Charles, 1971
Colbert, Tom, 1972
Taylor, Charles, 1975
Williams, Randy, 1975–76
Abaernathy, Mel, 1975–76
Nichols, Willie, 1976
Anderson, Greg, 1976–77
Myree, Craig, 1976–77
Grimes, Hamil, 1976–78
Small, Trevor, 1977

University of Pennsylvania, at Cheyney
Cheyney, Pennsylvania 19319

Coaches of Varsity Teams

O'Shields, William, 1956–63
Davis, Ira, 1967–68
Scott, John, 1968–70
Thorpe, Noah H., 1971

Men's Cross Country
O'Shields, William, 1956–63

All Pennsylvania State College Conference

Williams, Jimmy,[1] 1965
Jones, Charles,[2] 1966
Kennard, David,[3] 1966
Allen, Glenn,[4] 1966–68

[1] Williams, Jimmy—1965 Pennsylvania State College Conference 100-Yard Dash Champion
[2] Jones, Charles—1966 Pennsylvania State College Conference Shot Put Champion
[3] Kennard, David—1966 Pennsylvania State College Conference Long Jump Champion
[4] Allen, Glenn—Cross Country Pennsylvania State College Conference Champion; 1966 One- and Three-Mile Run

West Virginia State College
Institute, West Virginia 25112

Coaches of Varsity Teams

Men's Track
Cardwell, Mark, 1947–60
Price, Roderick, 1960–63
Wilson, James, 1963–66

Harris, D., 1964–66
Smiley, Jr., Glover L., 1983–Present

Women's Track
Smiley, Jr., Grover L., 1979–85

Cross Country
Smiley, Jr., Grover L., 1984–85

All West Virginia Intercollegiate Athletic Conference

Tucker, Sam
Harris, Michael
Pleasant, Ronald
Smiley, Jr., Glover L.
Early, Jerry
Taylor, Tyrone
Hairston, Kevin
Hairston, Mark
Curry, Sam
Tyson, Michael
Lester, Scott
Gilmer, Rodney
Davis, Ivory
Smith, Manuel
Savage, Bernard
Cunningham, Leon
Reid, Walter[1]
Lipscomb, William
Crummel, George[2]
Bethel, Antoine
Alcorn, James
Smith, Manuel

[1] Reid, Walter—1975 WVIAC Track Man of the Year
[2] Crummel, George—1973 WVIAC Track Man of the Year

Index

131